The Authors

C000080419

Kwasi Kwarteng is t⌐
Spelthorne, and is a mem⌐⌐ ⌐
Transport. He earned a PhD at Cambridge University
in History in 2000. He is the author of two previous
books. The first, *Ghosts of Empire* (Bloomsbury), deals
with the legacy of the British Empire, while the second,
Gridlock Nation (Biteback), looks at the politics of British
transport.

Priti Patel is the Member of Parliament for Witham.
She was educated at a comprehensive secondary school
in Watford and finished her formal education at the
University of Essex. She has worked in the communications industry for over ten years and until recently was
the Director of Corporate Communications at a major
international company.

Dominic Raab is the Member of Parliament for Esher
and Walton, and is a member of the Joint Committee
on Human Rights. A trained corporate lawyer, he has
also worked for the foreign office, and spent three years
as Chief of Staff to respective shadow Home and Justice
Secretaries. His first book, *The Assault on Liberty – What
Went Wrong with Rights* (Fourth Estate), criticised
Labour's approach to human rights.

Chris Skidmore is the Member of Parliament for
Kingswood, and is a member of the Health Select
Committee. He has worked as the Conservative Party's
Education Adviser and is a former Chairman of the
Bow Group. His first book, *Edward VI: The Lost King
of England* (Weidenfeld & Nicolson), was published in

2007. His second, *Death and the Virgin* (Weidenfeld & Nicolson), was released in 2010.

Elizabeth Truss is the Member of Parliament for South West Norfolk, and a member of the Justice Select Committee. She was brought up in Yorkshire, attending the local comprehensive school before going on to read Philosophy, Politics and Economics at Oxford. After working in the energy and telecommunications industry for ten years, she served as Deputy Director for the think-tank Reform.

All five contributors were elected as new Conservative Members of Parliament in the general election of 2010.

After the Coalition
A Conservative Agenda for Britain

Kwasi Kwarteng
Priti Patel
Dominic Raab
Chris Skidmore
Elizabeth Truss

After the Coalition
A Conservative Agenda for Britain

Biteback Publishing

First published in Great Britain in 2011 by
Biteback Publishing Ltd
Westminster Tower
3 Albert Embankment
London
SE1 7SP

ISBN 978-1-84954-158-9

10 9 8 7 6 5 4 3 2 1

A CIP catalogue record for this book is available from the British Library.

Set in Adobe Garamond Pro by Namkwan Cho
Printed and bound in Great Britain by
CPI Group (UK) Ltd, Croydon, CR0 4YY

Contents

Introduction

2010 proved a milestone in British politics. The formation of a coalition government ushered in a new politics of compromise. Two distinct parties put aside their differences to tackle an immediate priority, bringing the budget deficit under control. For the next four years, the political landscape will be defined by the ability of the coalition government to manage the current financial crisis, and to reduce public spending. The deficit has become the defining feature of the coalition.

Yet what will be the future of the coalition? Indeed, will it retain any purpose once the deficit is brought under control? In particular, what will become of the Conservative Party?

It is unlikely that the Conservative Party will fight for a further five years of coalition government in 2015. Labour may have lost the last general election, but it remains a harsh truth that, while David Cameron has become the first Conservative prime minister in thirteen years, John Major still remains the last head of a Conservative government.

The Conservatives are likely to fight for their own separate mandate, reinforcing their values. What that mandate will be and the ideas that will underpin it need to be defined now.

2010 also proved to be something of a watershed for the Conservative Party itself. Nearly 150 new Conservative MPs were elected, the largest single number of new members of the party since 1931. This has provided the party with new blood and a fresh face, for the first time in decades reducing the average age of a Conservative MP to below fifty. Many of the 2010 intake have been keen to make their impact felt on the party at an early stage, dominating select committees and taking active roles within the 1922 Committee. This group will be a powerful force, whose opinions and ideas will help define the Party, and have a wider impact on British politics.

In this book, five new Members of Parliament from this group, representing a spread of constituencies, have come together to identify today's challenges, and to explore ideas for the future to overcome them.

Politics depends on change. Politicians must constantly adapt to the needs of society and tackle new problems. As we enter the second decade of the twenty-first century, the Conservative Party must adapt to the challenges of modern society if it is to remain both distinct and relevant.

The book does not pretend to be exhaustive, but it tackles a range of important issues, not only for today but for tomorrow. These can only be met through restating our Conservative principles: that the future of Britain's prosperity lies in its liberal and free market values, while the welfare of its citizens must be directed towards greater individual responsibility.

Each chapter in this book is largely self-contained. They can be read, sampled from or even skipped over by the reader in whichever manner is preferred. Indeed, the main thrust of our analysis can be appreciated solely by reading this Introduction and our chapter on Values. Each chapter is concluded by a summary agenda giving key recommendations. These suggestions are summarised in the Book in Brief section at the end of the book.

Our belief is that Britain should strive to be among the most competitive and pro-business nations in the world. Within the context of a thriving economy, we should continue the reform of our public services. We need a new settlement for working families that reduces regulation for business and increases flexibility for parents. The wider relationship of Britain with the world and with Europe, in particular, is vitally important.

We begin by looking at the Conservative principles that we feel are relevant to today. We assert the paramount importance of fiscal responsibility. Without a prosperous country we can never achieve our goals in society or provide an adequate safety net for our most vulnerable citizens. The last thirty years of public debate in Britain has been dominated by left-wing thinking, particularly in education and society. Although there is a Conservative-led government, there still remains a left-wing consensus. Examples of this type of thought are found in 'identity politics' in which an individual's ethnicity or gender is seen as all important without any regard to the person. Statists have also 'annexed' family policy, claiming the means of progress is state involvement and institutionalised subsidy support. The same thinking has cramped any real discussion in education policy, where an egalitarian consensus has demonised the notion of academic rigour in state schools. Underpinning any debate about education is the notion of excellence and meritocracy leading to social mobility. The Conservative Party should reclaim the idea of social mobility and meritocracy to establish itself as a credible party of government.

The first part of the book looks at income and expenditure. Governments raise income through taxation, which comes from business enterprise and the private sector in general. We first look at issues of taxation, the role of the state in the economy, and implementing the best conditions for economic growth. This section also looks at the question of the environment within the wider context of economic growth.

As a consequence of the financial crisis of 2008, the United Kingdom faced the biggest deficit in its peacetime history. This deficit was £160 billion, since the government took in £540 billion and spent £703 billion in the fiscal year 2009–10.

This gap, known as the deficit, represented 12.8 per cent of national GDP. This proportion was contrasted to a figure of 3.3 per cent in Germany during the same period. The extent of the deficit was a consequence of Labour spending from 2001, when the then Chancellor, Gordon Brown, decided to accelerate public spending.

It is a major argument of this book that government spending across an economic cycle should, as a rule of thumb, never increase faster than the rate of economic growth in the country as a whole. To put this another way, the public sector should never grow faster than the private sector. Of course, during a slowdown, the so-called 'automatic stabilisers' will ensure that public spending increases faster than the economy but this should be an exception to the broad fiscal rule we have outlined. We need to wean Britain off its love of public spending and the sense of entitlement that has developed.

We propose a second fiscal rule of thumb, which is, in effect, a tighter restatement of Gordon Brown's 'Golden Rule' – that budgets should be balanced across a cycle. This in fact is what Keynes envisaged. Under favourable economic conditions, governments would run surpluses to be reinvested in the economy under more difficult economic conditions. Keynes never imagined, however, that a government would have to borrow money at a time of strong economic growth. This is exactly what happened between 2001 and 2007.

More generally, the widely oscillating nature of British politics, in which Labour governments spend only to run up huge deficits which Conservative governments then have to pare down, is very debilitating to the country. The Conservative Party has to win the wider argument about fiscal management. We almost succeeded in doing this in the run up to 1997, when Labour were forced to pledge to stick to the Conservative Party's spending plans. This discipline was abandoned after 2001. Conservative politicians need to win that argument a second time, and make it harder for subsequent governments of any political colour to spend as profligately as Labour did in the first decade of the twenty-first century.

We also believe that Conservatives should be more focused on what are called 'supply side' policies to boost economic growth. The history of the late twentieth century showed repeatedly that economies that had lower tax rates, like Japan in the 1950s and 1960s, Hong Kong in the 1970s and 1980s, Estonia and other Baltic states in the 1990s, grew at a faster rate than high tax economies. Cutting taxes improves the incentives for entrepreneurs.

A combination of fiscal discipline and greater incentives through the tax structure will, even in the medium term, give a country a more prosperous future than a regime of high taxes and excessive public spending. These obvious facts, it seems, need to be restated in every generation and the contributors to this volume are unabashed in their commitment to these ideas.

The second section of the first part of the book deals with public spending, more specifically the provision of public services. The three biggest slices of public spending are, in order: social protection, health and education. The second section on spending is necessarily focused on policy in these three areas.

To compete globally, we need vastly to improve education standards. Other countries are achieving not only better levels of literacy and numeracy. They are also equipping future generations with the high skill levels needed for the jobs of tomorrow.

We should place greater emphasis on school performance, rather than exclusively obsessing about pupil selection. For too long the British education debate has hinged on the quality of students attending a particular school – grammars v. Secondary Moderns on the right, 'banded entry' and lotteries on the left – rather than the quality of schools themselves. The 'poor quality of students' has been a veil behind which failing schools and failing teachers have hidden.

Of course we should give schools and students more freedom over entry criteria, but it is reasonable to expect more attention to be placed on competition between schools. We should increase quality by allowing profit making schools to enter the sector. There is also a wider cultural question about why British students are apparently less motivated and less 'academic' than overseas counterparts. The anti-success culture which is embedded in many schools and universities needs to be directly challenged. If 95 per cent of Japanese students are graduating schools at A Level standard, why isn't the same proportion of British children?

One of the major problems in British education is the number of students that cut options off too early.

For example, 50 per cent of comprehensive school sixth forms do not offer Further Maths A Level, which means that students aren't able to study maths or physics at a top university. The coalition government has reintroduced setting within schools. This initiative is to be welcomed, and should be extended. The most successful school systems in the world have an 'escalator' policy. This compels all students to reach the base level each year (at the risk of being held down a year), but also allows students to accelerate through the system. While there should be a core that continues to 18, as students get older, there should be more options available and those of high ability should be pushed forward. Bright students from low income backgrounds should have a 'college track' through the system, encouraged by scholarships and prizes.

Our public and social services face ever greater demands. We live in a society which is facing severe demographic pressure. In health and social care, an ageing population will require ever more complex services; in schools more pupils have specific needs requiring greater personalisation; in housing waiting lists remain interminable. It is clear however that the ability of the state to fund growing demands for social services may be pushed to breaking point.

The Conservative Party is fully committed to a National Health Service which is free at the point of delivery and accessible to all. However, this commitment does not mean that the NHS services should be trammelled by vested interests which have led to it becoming the third largest workforce in the world, employing more managers than doctors.

Healthcare reform is desperately needed because otherwise the NHS will simply go bust within a couple of decades. Demographic change, particularly the increase in life expectancy, will place a massive burden on its resources, 80 per cent of which are dominated by care for the elderly. We want to protect the NHS. To do this, however, we must look at how other countries have adapted to the increasing demand for healthcare.

The second axis upon which government acts is security. The first part of the second section of the book (part 3) concerns domestic affairs. We begin by looking at our justice system, and what we can do to regain the public's confidence in sentencing, prisons and control of immigration. We next look at what can be done to protect our civil liberties, and ensure a healthy pluralism among the voices in our media.

We believe that civil liberties were grossly eroded under the last government, and we do not see any inconsistency between adopting a tough penal policy and a more liberal approach to civil liberties. The principle can be very simply expressed. British justice should be firm but fair: we should allow the citizen the widest possible freedom within the law, but we should be very firm in our condemnation when the citizens steps outside that law.

Finally, we take a look at what we could do to create a more sustainable relationship between Scotland the rest of the United Kingdom.

The concluding part of the book (part 4) is concerned with Britain's position in the world, and treats foreign policy, our relations with the EU, and the provision for our security against external threats, namely defence.

Great Britain, because of her history, has played a significant role in global affairs during the last 300 years. Modern Conservatives are equally ambitious for Britain to 'punch above her weight' internationally and fulfil her historic role. In the current situation of international uncertainty, modern Conservatives believe that there should be strong and effective defence.

Providing for the security of its citizens against external threats is one of the first duties of any government. In the context of Britain's dire fiscal situation, more commitment should be made to protect levels of spending in defence, while at the same time maintaining a disciplined approach to costs.

Defence remains a paramount concern in the second decade of the twenty-first century. We only have to see British forces committed in theatres of war in Iraq, Afghanistan, and now Libya, to see how uncertain and changeable our world remains. Despite this, it has always been a contention of the Conservative Party that we should not be the policeman of the world. If Britain ever played such a role, this part had been relinquished at least as long ago as 1945. Modern intervention will always be undertaken on a mixture of humanitarian and strategic interests. But, it must reconcile ends and means – the most basic tenet of a credible foreign policy.

It would be naive always to commit Britain's armed forces to operations in another country on humanitarian grounds alone. Similarly, it would be an unrealistically cynical politician who only ever committed British forces to further our national interests in a narrow way.

Consequently, a pragmatic balance between humanitarian concerns and our national interests can be the only permanent principle upon which to base a foreign policy. To argue that we should never intervene on humanitarian grounds is cold hearted and, in the long run, detrimental to our national interest, as it would damage our reputation abroad.

The same pragmatism is adopted in this book in relation to questions concerning Britain's relationship with the EU.

It is a general assumption of the contributors to this book that younger Britons identify just as readily with the wider world as they do with the continent of Europe. Gap year students, young professionals and aspirant workers are just as likely to travel to Thailand, the United States or Australia as they are to go to Italy, or France.

This cultural phenomenon should shape our view of the EU. We remain committed to a Europe in which trade can flourish, but will be determined in our opposition to further political integration within the EU.

After the Coalition aims to be a general and broad statement of the Conservative solution to the problems of British politics. It is one of the first treatments of what a Conservative Party might look like in the wake of the first coalition government since the Second World War. We firmly believe that such a restatement of general ideas, across a wide range of policy, is necessary. The fact that the coalition government is *not* a Conservative administration means that a reassertion of the principles of the Conservative Party itself, as distinct from those of the government, should be made. *After the Coalition* is a contribution to that effort.

1. Values and Priorities:
A Return to Responsibility

The next hundred years look set to be the century in which the rest of the globe finally catches up with the west. Across the world, long poor nations have finally left behind socialist dogma. Instead they are applying liberal, conservative lessons, and reaping the rewards. They are opening up their markets, teaching their students, building new infrastructure, and saving much of their newfound wealth for still better futures.

Unfortunately, Britain seems to be heading in the opposite direction. Both as individuals and as a nation we have racked up ever greater debts, rather than savings. The nation of shopkeepers has become a nation of shoppers. Our infrastructure is crumbling, and seems to take decades to replace. Our students are falling behind in international league tables, while our health system struggles with an aging population. Millions of our most vulnerable remain trapped on benefits, while the only new jobs are taken by more entrepreneurial immigrants. Our influence in the world is constrained by the ever growing strength of the European Union.

These problems will not be solved with a new task force or more quangos.

What is needed is a new phase of the Conservative philosophy: Britain's historic respect for free markets, and the Conservative belief in individual responsibility.

The Thatcher reforms of the 1980s halted Britain's long twentieth century decline, but their work remains incomplete. While the British government no longer directly owns many of Britain's industries, its bureaucrats still exert enormous control through their new laws, quangos and regulations. The belief that markets need to be controlled by strong, central planning is still prevalent in Whitehall.

Worse, there still exist many industries which the government actively runs. As our population ages and our skilled workers become ever more important, our two leading industries are likely to be the government-run health and education sectors. As the last ten years have shown, simply giving either of these sectors more money has not been enough to stop them from sliding down the world rankings. The productivity increases of the private sector don't seem to have occurred in their public counterparts.

In Britain today, the word 'profit' remains a dirty word. We can never be a confident, entrepreneurial nation as long as our politicians shy away from 'competition'. The strange belief that public sector work is motivated exclusively through duty and that the private sector is driven solely by greed runs deep. Already, essential public sector reforms have been put at risk from the public's prejudice against markets.

We should not be too disheartened. Britain is well placed to benefit from the economic trends of the twenty-first century. We are a creative, cosmopolitan, English-speaking people. If we can take advantage of the new possibilities from the internet and the global mass market we can achieve great successes. But in order to seize these advantages we will have to be prepared to take more risks, to experiment and, ultimately, to compete.

As well as acquiring a greater sense of purpose, each of us will have to take more responsibility.

If we are honest, the government and its politicians have not set a very good example. For too long the State has spent more than it has brought in from taxes. Politicians have been too afraid of telling voters what they don't want to hear. They have tried to pretend that hard choices can simply be ignored. We can't really expect voters to make new sacrifices, unless we treat them as grown-ups in the decision making process.

Nobody can fully escape their background. Nevertheless, the Statist way of thinking is naive to focus wholly on the social causes of an individual's poverty. Individuals always have some choice. By creating systems that rob individuals of their autonomy, we are creating dependents of the state, unable to look after themselves.

The State cannot do everything. While the government can help, it can never fully solve any individual's problems. The NHS can't keep you healthy if you don't exercise or eat properly. No teacher can get you the right grades if you aren't prepared to work. The Benefits office can't find you a job if you aren't prepared to write a CV.

Part of this shift to greater personal responsibility will be financial. Individuals ought to save more for their future or ill health, rather than rely on the central state to do it all for them. Across the public sector we will need to see more use of personal budgets and individual decision making.

This additional responsibility is necessary to stop the government's costs from soaring out of control, but it should not be seen solely in terms of an added imposition.

Giving individuals greater responsibility is the first step to increasing their own freedom. Responsibility gives people the power to stand on their own, to solve their own problems, and to live the life they want to lead. Government should stand ready as a last resort. It should not be the first place to turn.

The coalition and this book

The authors of this book are fully supportive of the coalition government. Indeed, we believe that not only is the coalition essential in order to break the shackles of Labour's dangerous addiction to debt, but it makes and will continue to make real differences to the lives of millions. We are removing hundreds of thousands of the lowest paid workers from paying tax; immigration has been capped; we are beginning to reform the benefit culture that has wasted lives and crippled our public finances. In one year, the coalition has made real progress in undoing thirteen years of damage that Labour inflicted on Britain's finances.

Our mission is simple. We want to see David Cameron re-elected as a Conservative prime minister leading a Conservative government.

History teaches us that coalitions are never built to last. They serve a temporary need, often at times of crisis. Once that crisis has passed, they dissolve to become a chapter in the annals of political history. Likewise, we must understand that the current coalition is one which meets a temporary, but nevertheless important need, to pay off the fiscal deficit. Once this has been achieved, the coalition will have achieved its purpose. Political parties may once again be able to offer voters a choice between which party they believe should be entrusted to guide the future of Britain.

Many of the most popular policies of the coalition that resonate with the silent majority of the British public are in fact Conservative policies. Our values of rewarding those who work hard are reflected in Iain Duncan Smith's Welfare Reform Bill and Michael Gove's free schools and academies programmes. Theresa May understands the public's overwhelming desire that immigration be tackled fast and effectively.

We also believe that by 2015, as the Conservative Party, we will need to be able to distinguish ourselves from the coalition. We will need to be able to face the public and ask for another term, not as a coalition, but as a single party of government. To achieve this, we recognise that the most important task we have is to repair our broken economy.

Yet no government can simply rely on its past record; it must present a vision of the future and how it is determined to shape that future for the better. Above all, it must set out its vision in clear and simple terms to the public.

As Conservatives, we need to explain to the public what we would do differently from the coalition. And as Conservatives, we need to have the confidence in our own beliefs to establish a distinct platform of what a new Conservative government could offer.

In the second decade of the twenty-first century, we are not interested in preserving the divisions that wrecked the Conservative Party in the late twentieth century. We understand that the Conservative Party is a broad church that reflects many strands of political opinion, but what unites us is a belief in freedom. As we argue, there is nothing wrong with aspiring to a better life. Indeed it should be encouraged, rather than crushed in the interests of the State.

Conservative values

Under its current leadership, the Conservative Party has successfully shaken off negative associations and earned the right to be heard. Changes in the world give credence to the Conservative analysis. The development of technology has empowered people and groups at the expense of hierarchies and entrenched institutions. Globalisation has delivered increased prosperity, but regulation and intervention has created unease about windfall rewards. The egalitarian structures of post-war Britain are crumbling – unable to bear the weight of their own expectations. Conservatives need to be leaders in the progress of Britain, where our beliefs in markets, liberty, meritocracy, responsibility, and patriotism are translated to the modern era.

The new Left emerged in the 1960s and 1970s with a form of identity politics that grouped people together to form a rainbow coalition: women's groups, gay rights and black and minority ethnicity citizens. In contrast, the Right cherished the uniqueness of the individual and shared values over this static approach.

On entering government, Conservatives have found a maze of self-defeating processes and procedures warping the underlying values and convictions supposedly driving them. Child poverty targets, waiting lists, school results and climate change targets dominate departmental inboxes. These targets form the basis of a view which sees the individual as less important than the system which created them. Ministers are expected to pull levers on this energy-consuming machine to deliver a utopia in the wider world. But the utopia doesn't exist and, as Tony Blair found to his cost, the levers aren't connected to an outcome.

Meanwhile the things we value like beauty and merit are diminished in a world driven by systems and processes.

Managerialism has been very effective in parts of industry, driving down the costs of production in car manufacture and leading to more efficient farming practices. But it can only work up to a point. No system can fully replace the need for individuals to take responsibility for their own lives, their families, and doing their work well.

Debate on our criminal justice system centres on the economic outcome of the prisoner and how they can be managed through the system. People are now seen as a product of their background and experiences – not as free agents. Where there is no free will there can be no responsibility. This pervades our society: the leader of social services who believes a 'no-blame' culture should prevail; the teacher who knows that diluted qualifications will not benefit students, merely push up rankings in the league tables; the school child who writes a brilliant essay which the examiner is forced to mark down as it hasn't ticked the boxes on the mark scheme.

The rule of law has changed from clear principles and predictable rules to be applied by the courts in concrete cases, into a series of complex regulations which are themselves liable to obfuscation by further judicial legislation. Everywhere the right decision is obscured by the complexity of the system; government departments end up implementing policies they don't believe in, fearful that they will be judicially reviewed. Businesses who want to recruit staff are tied up by yards of red tape. A company won't hire candidates because it will be so difficult to fire them if they do not perform.

As well as failing to blame, the system fails to reward according to desert. Freely available Central Bank money has created windfall rewards that have been snapped up by the lucky. The baby-boomer generation, sitting on large amounts of equity in their houses reaped the benefits of inflation. The result is that the already skewed distribution of wealth has become more so. Bankers, lawyers and managers in major corporations have hidden behind 'innovative financial products' and opaque practices to cover up their subsidy from the rest of the economy. Risks that should have been borne by those who took them have been socialised by the government. In some cases directors' accountability to shareholders has weakened, dislocating pay from performance and wider scrutiny of the Board. A Victorian railway investor whose track failed to make money would have lost his shirt. A modern banker walks away with a golden handshake.

The culture of entitlement is not limited to those who claim welfare. From school children who are mollycoddled rather than inspired, to pensioners who are guaranteed that after thirty years of input into a pension pot, they can claim thirty years of pension. Risks have been taken away from the bearer and put on to a regulator, infantilising the bearer and protecting them from the impact of their own actions. Our society treats children like adults, and adults like children.

A society that fails to hold people to account and to reward or blame cannot promote merit. Instead it promotes a determinist attitude to the future: what will be, will be. Politicians have embraced the strand of popular culture that shows truculent distaste for intelligence and endeavour. In this culture, hard-working school children are dismissed as geeks, and celebrities are extolled. School pupils are encouraged to think that they have to secure a lucky break to become the next Cheryl Cole rather than work hard to achieve more substantial goals. A growing number of aspirational parents secretly tutor their own children. The system devalues endeavour and belittles important subjects like sciences and languages, promoting prizes for all and pretending that all subjects are 'equally valid'.

Since the pre credit crunch noughties, there has been less concern about just and fair outcomes. There was broad public support for the government spending more money, partly because many believed that the milk and honey would flow forever. Now there is less money to go around, questions of fairness and justice become acute. Yet politicians continue to react more slowly than public opinion to this new environment.

The economic system is not seen as meritocratic or fair. Altruism is damaged as we are forced into paying for others. Patriotism is dented by a lack of common feeling and a sense that we are not a cohesive society.

Human judgement and character should command a greater role in public life; not just in the case of politicians but also civil servants, community groups and business leaders. By strengthening the role and responsibility of the individual, we are helping them provide for others, their family, and their community. However, Conservatives should not be dogmatic about the structures in which people live, provided they are taking responsibility for themselves and their dependents. Conservatism has been caught up in defending traditional models of living as society moved on. For example, a married couples' allowance should apply equally to one-earner and two earner families with children under sixteen, irrespective of sexuality. In parts of our society this failure of responsibility became chronic. The riots of summer 2011 showed how fragile some elements of our society were, and how easily they could descend into utter lawlessness. The riots represented nothing less than our decades-long failure to pass on the ethic and culture of responsibility to all in our society, and in particular to our young. There has been a systematic failure in our schools, our justice system, our culture and our families. Simplistic theories of grievance and multiculturalism have been allowed to stand in place of holding the wrong to account.

Asking more of people necessitates greater transparency and individual accountability – social pressure to do the right thing. Senior public servants and business leaders should be as visible as politicians. Leaders should be encouraged to adopt an enlightened and far-sighted view of their responsibilities. Individuals who fail to deliver should be named and held to account.

We need not be defeatist. We can restore British values of hard work, fair play and responsibility. But to do so, any future Conservative government must be prepared to state and follow its own values. If Britain's historic values are good enough for newly growing Asian economies, they should also be good enough for Britain today.

SUMMARY AGENDA
- Individuals, organisations and governments need to take more responsibility for the success and failure of their own actions.
- We need to challenge today's cultural consensus that free markets, profit and competition are inherently bad. These virtues lifted Britain and much of the rest of the world out of poverty and into the modern era.

SECTION ONE

MAKING MONEY AND
SPENDING MONEY

2. Economy: The New Golden Rule

The current financial crisis has sharply illustrated debt's power to undermine nations' ability to control their own destiny. Governments may have deeper pockets than any individual, but they too cannot keep spending forever. Markets are only prepared to lend to any country so long as they believe it has the will and ability to pay them back. That will has looked less resolute in recent months.

On the continent, the Eurozone threatens to collapse as its elites struggle to meld together different cultures and welfare states under a single currency. Some countries such as Greece have been grossly irresponsible in their spending. Others, such as Ireland, were unlucky in suffering the fallout from the European Central Bank's bubble. Many are losing any ability to set their own taxes, and to decide what public services their governments should pay for. Every other objective is overtaken by the greater demand of avoiding an all-devouring financial crisis.

Meanwhile, the US political system is paralysed by arguments over the country's debt. Dangerous political games are played over extending the country's self-legislated debt ceiling, threatening to downgrade the US's credit rating and spread further chaos through the financial markets. Behind the short term arguments lie more fundamental disagreements over how to meet rising costs in the future.

The UK has been more fortunate than that most. Equipped with its own currency, it has avoided the traps ensnaring Ireland and Greece. The coalition government has ended the debt denial of Gordon Brown, and made the early, hard decisions to win back the credit markets' trust.

When New Labour came into power in 1997 the national debt was falling. Gordon Brown promised to be the 'Iron Chancellor' under which there should be no return to 'boom and bust.'[1] Instead the three new pillars of his macroeconomic policy would ensure a stable economy: a new independent central bank to manage demand, a new Financial Services Agency to watch over the banks and new fiscal rules to ensure prudence.

The first rule was the so-called Golden Rule: 'over the economic cycle, the government will borrow only to invest and not to fund current spending.'[2] Then there was the Sustainable Investment Rule, that 'public sector net debt as a proportion of GDP will be held over the economic cycle at a stable and prudent level.'[3] That prudent level, it was suggested, was a total debt of no more than 40 per cent of GDP.

Fourteen years later, the cumulative results of Brown's economic policy are clear to see. The independent central bank is accused of failing to spot an asset bubble, and

---

1   http://timesonline.typepad.com/comment/2008/09/boom-and-bust.html

2   http://webarchive.nationalarchives.gov.uk/+/http://www.hm-treasury.gov.uk/fiscal_policy.htm

3   http://webarchive.nationalarchives.gov.uk/+/http://www.hm-treasury.gov.uk/fiscal_policy.htm

having kept interest rates too low for too long funding a debt boom. The Financial Services Agency proved utterly incapable of regulating the banks adequately.

Worst of all has been the increase in debt. However you measure it, the UK's current fiscal position is dire.

At the start of the economic crisis, the UK found itself with the worst deficit in the whole of the G20, at 11 per cent of national income.[4] The UK's deficit is currently 10.4 per cent of GDP, worse than the troubled European economies of Portugal and Spain, at 9.1 per cent and 9.2 per cent respectively.[5] Estimates suggest that total debt will rise from 67 per cent to 77 per cent of GDP by 2015.[6] This is more than double the level in 2003.[7] Over this parliament, debt will likely increase by over £500 billion, or £19,000 for every household.[8] More disturbingly, the National Institute for Economic and Social Research estimates a failure to tackle current debt would leave a child born today with a tax bill of £200,000.[9]

No issue is more central to government than control of the public finances. Without budgetary responsibility, it is impossible to make the investments needed in our health, education or police systems. Taxes end up funding foreign bondholders rather than much needed

---

4   http://conservativehome.blogs.com/platform/2011/02/
     matthew-hancock-mp-we-can-ensure-growth-whilst-making-
     cuts-to-reduce-the-deficit.html

5   http://www.telegraph.co.uk/finance/economics/8473720/
     Why-the-UKs-deficit-is-only-half-the-story.html

6   http://www.businessweek.com/news/2010-11-09/u-k-s-total-
     debt-may-hit-10-trillion-pounds-by-2015-pwc-says.html

7   Rally Against Debt, 2011

8   Rally Against Debt, 2011

9   http://www.independent.co.uk/news/uk/politics/britainrs-
     quos-debt-the-untold-story-2025979.html

public investment. When trapped in debt, a country has little flexibility to cut taxes or spend more on benefits in difficult economic times.

It would be wrong to claim that budgetary irresponsibility is solely a province of the UK or parties of the Left. In the United States as well as Britain, deficits continued to expand even in times of economic growth. George Osborne's observation that they did not 'mend the roof when the sun was shining'[10] could equally apply to George W Bush's Republicans as Gordon Brown's Labour party.

If modern Conservatism is about encouraging greater responsibility, then we must make sure to increase government responsibility as well. It is not enough to trust politicians of any party to do the right thing. Instead we must put in place the right institutions to create a more sustainable fiscal policy.

In this chapter we will look at what such institutions might look like. How can we put in place a 'Golden Rule' that would not fail so utterly?

The legacy of John Maynard Keynes

All discussions of fiscal policy are dominated by the thought of John Maynard Keynes, and the impact of his ideas in the 1930s Great Depression. It turns out, surprisingly, that even in Keynes's own terms, we should be balancing the budget.

It is important to distinguish between what Keynes actually said, however, and how politicians over the years have chosen to interpret it. Keynes's *The General Theory of Employment, Interest and Money* is a subtle work, open

---

10   http://www.conservatives.com/News/Speeches/2010/02/
      George_Osborne_A_New_Economic_Model.aspx

to more than one interpretation. In the neoclassical economics that had dominated before Keynes, it was assumed that the only reason unemployment could exist in any economy was that prices and wages were 'sticky' – they would not adjust downward quickly enough to give everyone who wanted one a job. When faced with unemployment, the recommendation of classical economists was that the government should focus on removing obstacles to falling wages, such as trade union power or minimum wages laws. By contrast, Keynes argued that there were a variety of other mechanisms that could keep the total demand in any economy too low. If this 'aggregate demand' was too low, then unemployment would necessarily persist.

There are two methods a government can try to increase aggregate demand and restore an economy to full health. The first is through what is known as 'monetary policy'. The more money that is flowing through an economy, the more consumers buy, the more employers hire and companies invest. The second method is 'fiscal policy'. If the government can cut taxes, it leaves individuals with more of their own money which they then spend in turn in the wider economy. Alternatively, if the government increases its own spending, it can replace lost private sector demand itself.

It is important to understand the context of Keynes's recommendations in the 1930s. Worldwide, economies were not only in a severe recession but in what Keynes called a 'liquidity trap'. If interest rates are already zero, Keynes argued, it is impossible to lower them further and spur on the economy through monetary policy. Instead we have to make use of fiscal policy to boost aggregate demand: government should spend more and tax less.

As the years went on, these special circumstances were

often forgotten. Too often, the idea of Keynesianism became reduced to what economist Arnold Kling has called 'folk Keynesianism'[11] – the government must always keep spending to support the wider economy. The special conditions that made fiscal policy in one particular case more effective than monetary policy were forgotten. Politicians were understandably keen to have a theoretical backing for their eternal desire to spend more and tax less.

The other side of Keynesian thought, that in an economic boom government should cut spending and raise taxes, was similarly ignored. This fundamental imbalance has led to a long term tendency for national debt to rise across the developed world.

American economist and former adviser to President Obama, Christina D. Romer has argued that the roots of this irresponsibility began in the 1960s.

In the 1950s, governments largely thought of running a balanced budget as essential. Even under conditions of foreign war in Korea, or the creation of massive new entitlements such as the National Health Service, both President Truman and Clement Attlee trieed to keep their budgets balanced. Keeping such a balance was seen not just as morally right, but essential for long term economic growth.

By the 1960s however, governments began instead to believe that deficits could be a useful tool, promoting growth, decreasing unemployment and in time 'taking care of themselves'. In his 1964 Budget, President Kennedy argued that, 'The choice ... is between chronic deficits arising out of a slow rate of economic growth,

---

11   http://www.ideasinactiontv.com/tcs_daily/2006/01/how-thinkers-influence-us.html

and temporary deficits stemming from a tax program designed to promote fuller use of our resources and more rapid economic growth.'[12] President Johnson's 1966 Report argued that 'in focusing on balance of the economy, this policy strategy cannot give top priority to balance in the budget'.[13]

The results of this attempt at permanent stimulus were sadly predictable. The US budget remained in deficit 'in every quarter from [1965] to [1979], except for eleven quarters in the periods of strongest growth in the mid and late 1960s'.[14] The record on inflation was even worse. At the beginning of the Kennedy administration it was close to 1 per cent. By the end of the 1960s it was over 5 per cent. Over the course of the 1970s, it was over 10 per cent. Only a small part of this phenomenon was the fault of the oil price shocks of the decade.[15]

The UK fared no better. Aside from two solitary exceptions, the UK ran a deficit every single year between 1957 and 1987. In the 1970s, inflation averaged 13 per cent, peaking as high as 25 per cent in 1975.

The disaster of the 1970s ultimately broke the naive belief of Western governments that they could decrease unemployment by running permanent deficits. A revolution in economic thought, led by the work of Milton Friedman and Robert Lucas, reminded policymakers of Keynes's original, more nuanced policy recommendations. In the long run, it was now understood, fiscal policy did not work. Moreover its inevitable distortions

---

12   Romer, 2007, pg 9
13   Romer, 2007, pg 10
14   Romer, 2007, pg 14
15   Romer, 2007, pg 15

and lags meant that, even in the short term, monetary policy was a far more effective tool to tackle economic recessions. Government temptation to harm the long term health of the economy could be avoided by placing control of interest rates in the hands of independent central banks.

For a time, this economic settlement was remarkably successful. The painful reforms of Thatcher and Reagan put in place low inflation and relatively successful economies. Fluctuation in aggregate demand had dampened to such an extent that many began to speak of a 'great moderation'. In the 1990s, the governments of John Major and Bill Clinton slowly moved their economies towards surplus.

Unfortunately, the tranquillity was not to last. Lulled by the good times, Gordon Brown abandoned his early commitment to Conservative spending plans, and began to increase spending. In the US, George W Bush passed several rounds of tax cuts, a new entitlement in Medicare D and funded two new wars.

When the financial crisis of 2007 hit, the governments of the UK and US were ill prepared to deal with the problems ahead.

The costs of debt

Keynes showed us how, in the short term, a spending boost or spending taxes through increased debt can increase so-called aggregate demand.

In the long term however, increased debt is far from harmless to the wider economy.

The most obvious impact is, of course, in the increased interest bill it presents for future taxpayers. As debt is cumulative, this can build up quickly. Interest payments are already set to double from £30.9

billion in 2009/10 to £66.8 billion in 2015/16. This is more than the amount we spend on education, or the Defence, Transport, Home Office and Justice budgets combined.[16]

More damagingly, the cost of this interest bill is far from stable. Unforeseen events that cause the government to take on extra debt or a failure of trust in the bond market can quickly raise the cost of the interest paid on the debt. Every extra 1 per cent that the bond market forces the government to pay costs us an extra £6 billion.[17]

In the long term, as the government increases its own debt, interest rates in the wider economy correspondingly rise. This makes it harder for private sector companies and entrepreneurs to borrow their own funds to invest. The government's debt crowds out private sector investment. This was bad enough when the government debt was taken on to pay for its own investment; still worse when this debt was acquired to pay for current spending.

In order to pay for this debt, government will have little choice but to raise taxes. Not only are these taxes unfair to future generations, but they can also in themselves reduce future growth. The data seems to suggest that every 10 per cent GDP rise in spending cuts growth by 1–2 per cent a year.[18]

Increased debt costs money that could be used to pay for schools and hospitals; it reduces the country's resilience, and leads to higher taxes and lower growth. It should be avoided whenever possible.

---

16   Rally Against Debt, 2011
17   Rally Against Debt, 2011
18   Lilico, et al., 2009, pg 2

As Romer argues:

> the consequences of persistent deficits may only be felt
> over a very long horizon. Persistent deficits may crowd
> out useful investment so growth is slower. Such crowd-
> ing out may have enormous effects on standards of
> living over a century, but are unlikely to be noticeable
> over a decade or two.[19]

The problem with fiscal policy is that its misuse is always attractive for the politician. His horizons constrained by the five year electoral term, he is too tempted by the short term boost to our economy, ignoring the damage to the economy's long term health. Just as we have reduced the politician's discretion in monetary policy, we need to do the same in fiscal affairs.

What caused the deficit?

It is understandably convenient for those on the Left to blame the UK's current deficit problems on the finan-cial crisis. The crisis could not have been foreseen, this argument goes, and in any case was the fault of greedy bankers. In the context of a once-in-a-century financial emergency, the government had little alternative but to run up large deficits.

Indeed it is true that the financial crisis has not helped the UK's fiscal position. As the world's leading financial centre, the UK has understandably been hit worse than other countries by the collapse of the industry world-wide. However this is only part of the reason for the position in which the UK now finds itself. Our current

---

19   Romer, 2007, pg 26

problems are just as much the failure of Gordon Brown's Golden Rule as his regulatory system.

Over the course of this decade, the amount the government spends has significantly increased as a proportion of the economy. In 2000 government spending was around 36.8 per cent of GDP. In 2010, it was 47.1 per cent.[20] Even this might be an understatement since, according to the OECD, spending is now 51 per cent of GDP.[21]

In the early years of this new century, the New Labour government began an ambitious programme of government investment. The government argued that the public services had suffered from decades of under-investment. Large new spending promises were created: Building Schools for the Future, the cutting of waiting lists in the NHS, vast new investments in the railways. This was the first surge.

Ideologically, you may agree or disagree with New Labour's diagnosis for the need for more investment. Whatever the underlying value of public spending, the critical point is that Gordon Brown did not match increases in spending with corresponding increases in taxation. He gambled that there was no harm in a moderate deficit, as economic growth was projected to continue indefinitely. After all, hadn't he tamed boom and bust?

Political weakness in the Conservative Party meant that there was a failure to tackle this spending.

A second surge of spending came in the wake of the financial crisis. Tax revenues collapsed, as it turned out

---

20   HM Treasury
21   h t t p : / / w w w . o e c d . o r g / d o c u m e n t / 6 1 / 0 , 3 3 4 3 ,en_2649_34573_2483901_1_1_1_1,00.html

that the UK was simply not as rich as everyone believed. However, the New Labour government refused to cancel the spending projects it had already planned which, of course, were originally based on far more optimistic assumptions about Britain's economy.

This was not an inevitability, but a political choice. Germany, for example, is all too aware of the dangers of loose monetary policy and debt in general. Having struggled with increased deficits ever since the reunification of West and East Germany, Germany's leader, Angela Merkel, made a different choice when the financial crisis hit in 2007. In 2007, the UK ran a deficit of -2.8 per cent and the US -2.9 per cent. Germany, by contrast, ran a surplus of 0.3 per cent. Even at the worst moment in the crisis in 2009 when the UK's deficit was over 11 per cent, Germany's deficit was only 3 per cent. Its overall debt is expected to increase by no more than 10 per cent to around 52 per cent in 2012 – compared to the doubling of the UK's debt.[22] While Germany did not avoid the pain of the financial crisis entirely, the experiment with austerity does not seem to have harmed its economy. On the most recent reports, Germany is experiencing rapid growth, 3.6 per cent in 2010 – the fastest seen since reunification.[23]

It is arguable that in 2007 the Western economies were once again experiencing what Keynes called a 'liquidity trap', in which monetary policy is ineffective. The responsibility for supporting the economy falls on fiscal policy. According to Keynes, we should allow bene-

---

22   http://www.oecd.org/document/61/0,3343 ,en_2649_34573_2483901_1_1_1_1,00.html
23   http://www.ft.com/cms/s/0/37f5e88e-1e29-11e0-bab6-00144feab49a.html#axzz1LaXjP6vw

fit payments to rise and taxes to fall, while undertaking programmes of public investment to increase aggregate demand.

But such a programme only accounts for a small amount of this second surge. Perhaps 33 per cent of the increased costs came from changes to the tax and benefit bills, and another 6 per cent from the spending rise in public investment. A further 5 per cent of the change came from higher interest payments. The other 56 per cent of the spending was a simple result of the government spending money it didn't have on the public sector, planned in earlier, more benign years. [24] This is not at all what Keynes meant by fiscal policy. The Left have elevated Keynes to the status of a household god, but his fiscal policy was more conservative than radical.

But how was this increase in debt even possible? Wasn't this exactly what Brown's Golden Rule was supposed to avoid?

Fixing the Golden Rule

No rule can stop a government determined to spend more than it earns. Nevertheless, well designed rules can make such decisions more transparent, and alter the terms of any political debate. One reason that Britain's debt grew for so long is that it became too easy to see constant growth in spending as a natural law, and to vilify any diversion from this as 'cuts'.

One suggestion that has increasingly been suggested is the notion of a 'debt cap', the idea that Parliament should legislate a hard limit to the amount of debt the country could take on. If the government ever needed to raise more money, whether it be for day to day spending

---

24   Lilico, et al., 2009, pg 10

or to meet the needs of a national emergency, it would have to come to Parliament to declare its reasons.

In practice, the record of debt caps overseas has not been an encouraging one. Governments have all too easily simply raised them when they needed more funds. When they did not, as we see in the example of the US in the summer of 2011, the ensuing political arguments have threatened economic and financial disaster.

Instead, we would look to create a new rule enforcing a balanced budget. Now, this rule would not be simplistic or forget the lessons of Keynes – it would take into account the fluctuations of the economic cycle and the need for investment – but in the medium term, the government's books should balance.

Indeed, fundamentally, the principle behind the Golden Rule remains strong. What we are suggesting is a tighter restatement of the rule, maintaining its strengths while doing away with the loopholes that allowed Gordon Brown to increase spending in the way he did.

The Golden Rule attempts to safeguard the two reasons why a government might legitimately wish to take on extra debt. When a recession hits, the government may wish to borrow to manage demand, but when the economic good times arrive again it must pay back this extra debt and start saving for the next recession. In the long run, the government might wish to borrow in order to fund its investment programmes. It doesn't seem fair for taxpayers today to pay all the costs of infrastructure that will mostly be enjoyed by future generations.

There are two crucial ambiguities that, in practice, stopped this from working effectively. It was neither clear exactly what counted as the beginning or the end of the economic cycle, or what the precise difference between spending and investment was.

Let us take each case in turn.

Fiscal policy is not, as Folk Keynesianism suggests, necessary as a permanent stimulus to ensure economic growth and that unemployment is kept down. Neither is it necessarily the best way in which to manage aggregate demand. Today's macroeconomics suggests a variety of unconventional methods of monetary policy that can succeed in stimulating the economy, even when we can no longer manipulate interest rates. Perhaps the most effective stimulus we've seen in the last years has not been Obama's fiscal stimulus or Alistair Darling's VAT cut, but Ben Bernanke's quantative easing. It is quite consistent to cut back the spending of the State while maintaining demand through loose monetary policy – that is more or less the economic strategy of Britain today.

However, there does still remain some role for fiscal policy. When an economy suffers from recession, consumers spend less and workers lose their jobs. The effect of this is that tax receipts go down, while spending on benefits goes up. If the government makes no other changes, the inevitable result is an increase in the deficit. Conversely, when an economy booms, tax receipts increase while spending decreases. These are known as the 'automatic stabilisers' in the economy, and are the core of Keynesian thinking.

The objective of our fiscal policy, then, should be to maintain enough of a surplus in the good years to allow these automatic stabilisers to operate. Further stimulus can be the responsibility of monetary policy.

The problem with the Golden Rule is that the very notion of an 'economic cycle' remains an abstract proposition. It is difficult enough with hindsight to locate when a new cycle began, and next to impossible to predict such an occurrence. Instead of this retrospective process, it would be better to base our judgment on the idea of trend growth. The best way to stop political manipulation of the number is to give an independent body such as the Office for Budgetary Responsibility the job of determining what they believe it to be. As a guide, the UK economy has broadly grown at a rate of 2 per cent a year for decades. Our new Golden Rule should be that if the economy is growing faster than this, then the likelihood is that we are in a boom and should either be in or transitioning towards surplus.

The second ambiguity comes in the difference between spending and investment. On a vague enough definition, as accountants have long known, nearly anything can count as investment. Is increasing the wages of teachers an increase in current spending, or is it an investment in our children's future?

In any case, we should be careful to distinguish between two different types of investment.

Many people take out a loan to buy a car – but that not does make a car an investment. In the same way, the benefits of a hospital come over many years, but it is not the same thing at all as a carpenter investing in new tools to make him more productive.

Politicians often argue that we should take on more debt now to increase growth and tax revenue in the future. Politicians on the Left and the Right argue that investment in road, rail, education and benefits for the poor will more than pay for itself in the long term. Raising taxes to balance the budget is short sighted, argue some on the Right, as it ignores the idea that tax cuts can pay for themselves by inspiring more work.

There clearly is something to this. Some tax cuts do indeed end up generating more revenue than they cost.

Infrastructure is important, and can fundamentally improve the way the economy works.

The problem is not that effects don't exist, but that they are necessarily unpredictable. Nobody can really say any development will affect the future economy. We shouldn't have to rely on future projected tax revenues that might never arrive to fund developments today. It is not worth running a higher deficit for such speculative gains.

It is true that this is a highly cautious approach, but history seems to show that governments cannot be trusted with the power to borrow otherwise. Just like an individual, if the country wants to invest then sometimes we have to scrimp and save rather than stick it on the credit card. If in the 1940s the UK could set up the NHS while balancing the budget, then the UK can balance the budget again today.

That doesn't mean that the government shouldn't make any investments at all. Indeed, there is a good case to make that the government should be investing far more. There is no technical reason why 40 per cent of GDP is the level of debt that the UK should be aiming at. In truth, the UK level of total debt has always been far beyond this when liabilities for pensions, PFIs, the bank bail outs and semi-autonomous bodies such as Network Rail are included. One recent estimate by Brooks Newmark MP suggested that these liabilities totalled as much as a further £1,395 billion (or 100 per cent of GDP).[25]

The far more important point is that this debt should not grow uncontrollably. The best way to achieve this is with maximum transparency.

---

25   Newmark, 2009

UK investment has long lagged behind its other OECD competitors. Another Policy Exchange report compiled what it believed to be the minimum level of adequate investment in UK infrastructure to deal with coming challenges such as climate change, and came up with a colossal total of £434 billion.[26]

In order to fund these developments, and other long term infrastructure needs such as schools and hospitals, the UK should begin by exploring new means for raising capital. Innovative new financing schemes allow the government to raise far more money from the private sector to pay for new hospitals or railways. The important point is to make sure that government can meet the interest payments for these new debts without creating new deficits. There is a significant difference in borrowing to purchase an asset, and borrowing to fund current spending.

The creation of such deals of course runs the risk of manipulation of the books. Again, we should extend the responsibilities of the OBR. To begin with, we should use one of these bodies as the arbitrator of what a government can count as spending and what it can count as investment. In addition, we should charge it with producing an annual report stating out the full debt position of the UK government. If the government is taking on debts for the future, then we should at least have a better idea of what they are so we can judge the relative risks.

Just as an independent central bank took the politics out of monetary policy, we should make use of a strengthened Golden Rule and the new Office for Budgetary Responsibility to take some of the politics

---

26   Helm, et al., 2009

out of fiscal policy. Only then can we ensure that the deficit catastrophe of the last administration never occurs again.

SUMMARY AGENDA

- Over the course of an economic cycle, Britain should run a balanced budget. We should never be running persistent deficits when the economy is growing faster than 2 per cent a year, its long run trend.
- The Office for Budgetary Responsibility should be the final arbitrator for what government spending is counted as investment. It should release an annual report setting out Britain's full debt commitment, including its pension commitments, PFI deals and so on.

3. Business: Enterprise Britain

In the long run, few things matter as much as economic growth for national strength and prosperity. It is growth that allows us to live longer and healthier lives, to support the poor, to pay for public services and develop the new technologies we need to clean up the environment. Despite recent claims to the contrary, the evidence is that growth makes us happier as well as richer.[27] As Nobel laureate Robert Lucas once famously said, 'Once you start thinking about economic growth, it is hard to think about anything else.'

Despite its central importance, academics still do not understand exactly what causes growth. Economists can make recommendations about policies that are likely to be beneficial, but modern economies are far too complex to ever fully understand. Many factors that deeply affect a country's growth rate remain beyond the control of governments. No politician can micromanage the progress of a country's culture, science or technology.

What we do know is that since Industrial Revolution in the nineteenth century, Britain and other leading

---

27 Economic Growth and Subjective Well-Being: Reassessing the Easterlin Paradox, Justin Wolfers & Betty Stevenson, 2008

countries have grown at around 2 per cent a year. Other countries have at times grown much faster – usually through what is known as 'catch-up' growth, adopting technology that has already been designed elsewhere.

Small differences in the growth rate compound, causing significant differences to human welfare in the long term. An economy that grows at 2 per cent per year will double its size in 35 years, an economy that grows at 3 per cent will double in just 25 years. After 20 years, the average person in an economy that grows at 2.75 per cent rather than 2.5 per cent would earn an extra £1,250 a year.[28]

One of the difficulties in increasing growth is the complexity in simply measuring it. Without hindsight, it is almost impossible to distinguish between a long term improvement in the working of an economy and the short term boom of an economic cycle. National statisticians face an almost impossible task in trying to decide how much growth in salaries represents growth in wealth and how much represents inflation. How many horses is a Lexus Prius worth? What would a Victorian lord pay for an iPhone? There is no real answer to such questions.

What we can say is that the history of growth postwar in the West approximately divides into three stages. Western economies grew fast in the decades after the Second World War, taking advantage of technologies that had been developed earlier. By the 1970s however, growth across the world had slowed.

The limits of government-run economies becoming clear, the UK and the US embarked on a series of what we might term 'neoliberal' reforms. Taxes were cut,

---

28   Elphicke, 2011

inflation was tamed and inefficient government monopolies privatised. Although this did not succeed in fully returning us to the golden age of post-war growth, it did allow the UK and the US to grow relatively faster than their competitors.

Now, thirty years later, we are once again facing a long term challenge to our growth rate. In the wake of the financial crisis, our economy has slumped. The Treasury and the Office for Budgetary Responsibility (OBR) have cut their estimates of the UK's underlying growth rate. In 1999, the Treasury estimated our underlying growth rate at 2.5 per cent.[29] By 2014, the OBR now predicts it will be just 2.0 per cent, partly as a result of demographic changes.[30]

The challenges of globalisation mean that we are facing more competitors than ever before. Progresses in technology seem ever harder to make, as we develop more and more specialised technologies. We have already reaped all the easy gains of earlier advances. Some commentators, such as economist Tyler Cowen, even argue that we have reached a 'Great Stagnation', in which it will become ever harder for the West to grow.[31]

The situation is, if anything, worse than this in the UK. In recent years, our economy has become ever more dominated by financial services, an industry that looks set to struggle in coming years. The current rapid payment of the deficit, while necessary, makes it even more important for the private sector to be able to easily grow and take up the slack.

In other words, there is a real risk of our economy losing momentum. If we do nothing, growth may stagnate.

---

29   Diggle, et al., 2010
30   Elphicke, 2011
31   Cowen, 2011

While there is no one measure that can guarantee an improved growth rate, there are many different policies that we can pursue to help. In this chapter we focus on what measures we can take to make it easier for businesses and, crucially, entrepreneurs, to grow the economy.

The changes we need, however, are as much cultural as technocratic, and it is here that we begin.

Corporatism and the free market

Britain, once a nation built on trade and commerce has become risk-averse, suspicious of profit and work shy. Over the past century we have seen creeping state regulation and monopolistic practices replacing a genuine free market. Many large corporations have become 'too big to fail' and have been bailed out by the government.

World Bank research shows that over the last year Britain has lost ground when it comes to the ease of starting a business and the ease of paying taxes. Meanwhile, increased employment, workplace and specialist regulation have made it harder to manage the day to day aspects of business. Between 2007 and 2010 there were over 100,000 people working for quangos at a cost of over £40 billion. The intricate web of such bureaucracy remains hard to navigate for small businesses and start-ups in particular. This has meant that only the largest businesses are able to deal with this complexity. We have moved to 'survival of the fattest'.

We are in the grip of a culture that seeks to avoid every small risk, from the splinter in the floor to the overly hot coffee cup, and yet still manages to miss major risks like the entire financial system collapsing. In fact this has created a failure to properly understand risk and the connection between risk and reward. Corporate complexity and the disconnection of funding and operation have created 'arms lengths' relationships, where risks end up being concealed.

Risk used to be held by the entrepreneur, who would lose everything if the mine didn't contain any gold or the railway line failed. Now, it has been socialised. Northern Rock, whose business model was flawed, took excessive risk without retaining sufficient levels of capital. When it became the first British bank since 1866 to experience a run, the government could not find a buyer and therefore took on the credit risk of the bank itself.

Furthermore, the roles of owner and manager have become confused. Senior corporate officers are no longer seen as functionaries to carry out the will of the board. Owners and shareholders face the risks of management errors but have failed to properly hold managers to account. The fund managers and financial analysts who monitor board activity likewise have little incentive to ensure decent management principles. There has been much short term manipulation of financial results to drive up bonuses and short term corporate performance.

While individuals would, in order to make serious money, previously have had to create wealth through innovation and hard work, it is now possible to qualify as a corporate lawyer, a banker or work your way to the top of a public company and claim the rewards that were once reserved for entrepreneurs. Real chief executive pay rose by 8 times between 1986 and 2010 in the UK; in the US it rose by 6 times between 1989 and 2010. Between 1999 and 2009 the ratio of CEO to employee pay in the UK has risen from 47 times to 128.

The most extreme examples can be seen in the banking

sector, where large ill-understood risks were taken, underwritten by the State. The reckless actions of banks were, in effect, failed business decisions. However, they were business decisions in which the rewards were private, but risks were public. This fundamental distortion was reflected in the excessive salaries of executive and senior staff.

The public sector has copied this bad practice. We have a large 'twilight sector' of organisations like Network Rail, the BBC and univserity vice chancellors, which rely on guaranteed streams of public money. However their senior executives are paid 'commercial salaries' in recognition of the competition for their skills from private sector, commercial organisations. The Director General of the BBC's total annual remuneration is £696,000 higher than the prime minister's salary. These executives, however, are effectively civil servants, using public money to provide public services. The risks of losing their job are very low and they should be paid a salary that reflects this salient fact. Like the Civil Service, salaries for these jobs should be capped much nearer the level of the prime minister. The levels of pay for such figures are not reflective of differences in talent, skill or work level, but rather are artificially distorted.

In order to rehabilitate capitalism, people have to have confidence that the system delivers people their just deserts. A new corporate ethos is required where only those bearing risk receive rewards or, if salaried, are paid in line with their talents. There should be much more transparency about how salaries are determined.

We need to shift our moral perspective. Making an honest profit should be seen as a good thing, while rent seeking from the State should be regarded as a bad thing.

Tax

As the current debt crisis has shown, the British are not very good at saving – but this is as much a result of our tax system as our culture. Instead of taxing people on the investments they make, the jobs they provide, or the income they bring in, we ought to move more to a system which taxes spending or things we don't like, such as pollution.

Most industrial countries take between 30–50 per cent of their national income in taxation. The UK still lies in this range, although under Gordon Brown it has slowly increased its percentage and shifted to a more high spending, high tax European model economy. At present, it is far too easy for governments to earn more money through steadily increasing tax brackets, not properly indexed for inflation.

Economic research suggests that for every 10 per cent increase in the size of the government, the rate of growth slows by between 0.5–2 per cent.[32] Cutting back the size of the governments creates the room for business to grow. A World Economic Forum report suggested that the UK ranked 95th worst out of 139 countries for the problematic 'effect and extent of taxation'.[33]

Ideally, a system of taxation should be as simple as possible. Simplicity makes it easy for individuals to calculate their own tax bill. For the government, a simpler tax system makes it easier to spot fraud, reduce the perverse consequences of taxes or correct the mistakes which occur in working out our tax bills.

The current UK tax system contains many complexities which no longer serve any constructive purpose.

---

32   Lilico, et al., 2010
33   Elphicke, 2011, pg 2

Complexity has massively expanded in recent decades – Tolley's Yellow Tax Handbook grew from 4,998 pages in 1997 to 11,520 pages in 2010.[34] Tax administration now costs the economy over £5 billion a year.[35]

The recent Mirrlees Review by the Institute for Fiscal Studies offered a good template for what a long term reform of the tax system could look like, simplifying its structure and encouraging more saving.

As the review recommended and the government has indicated it will look into, the most obvious current anomaly is the division between Income Tax and National Insurance. Originally, these two taxes served very different purposes and worked on different principles. Those differences have now all but disappeared. National Insurance is now an insurance scheme only in name. Merging the two taxes would increase policy transparency, reduce complexity and remove the distortions which occur due to the interplay of the two rates.

A priority for tax reform should be reducing Corporation Tax. Research by the OECD suggests that by far the most harmful taxes for growth are corporate income taxes, followed by personal income taxes. Best are taxes on consumption and property, such as our current VAT.[36]

Corporation Tax is often misunderstood, particularly by the Left. A corporation is not a person – it cannot pay any tax. Instead, any increased tax bill is passed on either to its shareholders, its workers or its customers. Even if a left-wing politician did wish to tax the rich more, it would

---

34   Diggle, et al., 2010, pg 13

35   Boys Smith, et al., 2008, pg 5

36   http://freethinkingeconomist.com/2010/03/25/while-i-do-hate-the-argument-from-authority/

be far better to do this directly with increased income or consumption taxes rather than the blunt instrument of Corporation Tax. In today's global market, companies have to compete to be an attractive venue for investment. Already the coalition government is committed to lowering the rate of corporation tax by 1 per cent a year. In today's turbulent economic environment, we would do better to accelerate this pledge, immediately lowering it to 23 per cent in the 2012 budget. There would be a onetime cost to this of around £6 billion.

Finally, it is worth considering the marginal rates in a tax system. Each tax increase has two effects on revenue: it brings in more money from the increased tax rate, but less money from people trying to avoid the tax by giving up the activity. It is possible for the impact of the second effect to outweigh the first. If the tax rate on marginal income continues to increase, it eventually becomes no longer worthwhile to work more. Due to the complexities of our current tax system, some of the poorest currently face marginal tax rates as high as 90 per cent.[37]

The rich are even more sensitive to such changes. While it may not seem fair, the rich find it far easier to arrange their accounts to best advantage for tax purposes or, in extremis, emigrate out of the country altogether. The recent rise of the top rate of Income Tax to 50 per cent in the medium term is unlikely to raise any money, and should be reversed. Research by the Adam Smith Institute calculated that over ten years it could actually lose the Treasury as much as £640 billion.[38]

The cuts in the top rate in the 1980s did not reduce the revenue the Treasury took in Income Tax; they

37   Diggle, et al., 2010, pg 12
38   Young, 2011, pg 25

actually increased it. In 1979, the top 1 per cent of taxpayers faced marginal rates of 80 per cent and paid 11 per cent of the total income tax take. By 1997, they paid rates of only 40 per cent, but contributed 21 per cent of the income tax revenue, double the proportion they paid in 1979.[39] When Ireland reduced its corporation tax rate from 38 per cent to 12.5 per cent, revenues increased by 24.3 per cent a year.[40]

A less visible but often yet more costly form of taxation is regulation. The government's own figures suggest that the costs of regulation cost the economy around 10–12 per cent of GDP. That's over £100 billion a year, or a bigger burden on the economy than income tax.[41]

Most regulation is introduced with good intentions, even if it is created only to solve short term political problems. However, all too often the proponents of the regulation do not really quantify or predict the bureaucratic costs of adding in extra regulation. An economy dominated by paperwork is an economy that moves slowly.

The costs of some regulation are clear to see, in particular with regard to small business. By putting restrictions on who they can hire, what they must be paid and what time off they must be granted, we make it much harder for small companies to thrive. In effect, we are handing unfair advantages to large corporations who can afford to pay these extra expenses.

None of these changes to the tax system will be easy, from a political or a technical point of view. There will be significant complications in implementation, and

---

39   Young, 2011, pg 10
40   Elphicke, 2011, pg 3
41   Ambler, et al., 2010, pg 1

inevitably many short term losers. Nevertheless, in the long term, the UK needs to move to a smaller state, funded by smaller taxes based on consumption and carbon rather than savings and income.

Planning

In the aftermath of the Second World War, the UK government began a fifty year experiment with nationalisation. Believing that government planning was far more efficient than the chaos of free markets, the government nationalised sectors as diverse as health, transport, energy, and heavy industry.

This experiment was not a success. Across the world, economies discovered that government-run monopolies were unable to innovate. It was found that they could not reduce costs or be as responsive to customers as companies which operated under the discipline of free markets. Perhaps the most important improvement to the working of the UK economy in the last thirty years was the privatisation programme introduced by the Thatcher government.

Despite its mixed reputation, privatisation has been an almost unqualified success. New telecoms and energy markets have given consumers far more choice as well as cheaper bills. Productivity improvements in private sector utilities such as the water companies have far outstripped counterparts still left in government hands. Passenger numbers on the privatised railways have soared, while a new era of budget airlines has made flying affordable to all. One study showed that operating costs decreased each year at a rate of 3.7 per cent in the water industry, 4.1 per cent in sewerage, 6.5 per cent in the transmission of electricity, 6.8 per cent in electricity distribution, and 9.1 per cent in the transportation of gas.[42]

There is however one area of the UK economy that still hasn't been liberalised: its land system.

Before 1947, Britain ran a more or less laissez-faire system. If you owned land, you could build on it. After the 1947 Town and Country Planning Act, it became necessary to seek government permission to develop any land. Land was allocated for different purposes under zoning laws. While arguably this has helped preserve Britain's Green Belt and its historic buildings, the effects on growth have been disastrous.

Restrictive planning laws affect nearly every area of the economy. They make it harder for businesses to build new shops, offices or factories. They drastically drive up the cost of housing, and make it harder for workers to move and reallocate across the country.

Their effects are still worse in what increasingly seems to be the heart of our future economy: our cities.

In the old economy, a country's wealth was often based around its industrial centres: the textile mills of the North or the car companies in Detroit. These days, in our service-based economy, our prosperity depends on the workers themselves. The closer we can pack so-called knowledge workers together, giving them the potential to mingle and network, the faster an economy grows. One study suggests that each time you double the size of a city, each person working in it becomes 15 per cent more productive.[43] Across the world, more than half the

---

42   Selzer, 2000

43   http://www.nytimes.com/2010/12/19/magazine/19Urban_
West-t.html?_r=2

world's population now lives in cities, with an extra 5 million joining them each month.[44]

Our current restrictive planning system makes it hard to build in London or the surrounding area. It places limits on the heights buildings can reach, and allocates lands to purposes that could be more productively undertaken elsewhere. There are huge opportunities for gain: a hectare of agricultural land in the South East is worth around £7,000; a hectare with planning permission for housing worth over £3 million.[45] The current costs for both industrial and office space in the UK are among the highest in the world.[46] The more people we can fit into our urban areas, the richer our country will become. Greater London is more than 50 per cent more productive than the rest of the UK.[47]

The costs of our restrictive planning system are not only felt in terms of growth. By making it hard to move, our planning system helps entrench unemployment and poverty. The continual rise in house prices transfers money from the young to the old. Living in concentrated settlements such as cities is better for the environment, but our planning system makes this hard, increasing sprawl and pollution.

While the coalition has made good progress on simplifying the system, there is still more that could be done. There is no need for such strict criteria over land use and categories of land. At present, planning is decided as part of a top-down process, in which residents and local

---

44   Glaesar, 2011, pg 1

45   Leunig, 2007, pg 4

46   Evans, et al., 2007, pg 18

47   http://www.ft.com/cms/s/0/d6074404-48f5-11e0-af8c-00144feab49a.html#axzz1G63J9QYT

authorities feel that they are spectators. Planning should be something local communities do, not have done to them.

The Localism Bill is delivering more powers to local communities, with a New Homes Bonus which will encourage councils to build in their local areas. However, we should continue to increase local responsibility in the tax system. At the moment, when new development leads to increased tax revenues, this money is simply redistributed away by central government. This does not give local councils much incentive to pursue sometimes politically difficult building projects.

At the same time, local communities should also have greater say over which land they wish to preserve for generations to come. Not all land can be considered as a simple category, or classified with a label, and yet there are regular incidences where land which a community values the most is considered for development. The planning system must sustain the local democratic checks to ensure communities can preserve areas of local beauty. Green Belt status should be given greater value that it currently has. Rather than being a line on a map, more needs to be done to create 'living' green belts, marked out by more nature reserves, woodland walks, parks and allotment sites. In order to legally protect parts of a local community's most valued land, certain green belt sites should be given greater protection and opened up, along similar lines to National Parks and Forests.

The planning system must reflect the wider value of a building or operation that are not captured by the immediate market value. At present there is little reward to developers to develop a site in a way that is innovative or beautiful if it does not tick all the boxes on the planning guidelines. Locally elected decision makers should be able to use their judgement about the beauty of a building, its relation to our traditions and its contribution to society. There should be a market mechanism to enable trade-offs for near neighbours of developments as in France where electricity generators will offer free electricity to those who live nearby.

Our current centralised planning system makes it harder for the market to work efficiently, or new businesses to develop. At the same time, local communities feel that they are powerless in protecting the most valued areas of natural beauty. The current system is simply too bureaucratic to allow useful conversation between residents, councils and developers, creating a system that is far more adversarial than it needs to be. By sustainably reforming the system, we can ensure the right balance between the needs of newcomers and existing residents, businesses and the environment.

Infrastructure
Good infrastructure is essential to the economy as a whole, opening up new markets and allowing investors to more efficiently operate. New networks in transport, energy and communications radically change the way an entire economy works. Often the sheer scale of funding required, or difficulties in charging users when the work is finished, means that such investment projects require funding from central government.

The UK government, however, has traditionally prioritised the short term over the long term needs of our economy. Our infrastructure remains poor compared to our international competitors. International bodies such as the World Bank have complained that infrastructure remains inadequate and should be a significant priority investment.[48] According to the CBI, 70 per cent of senior business figures judged UK infrastructure to be poor and 85 per cent agreed that this had an impact on their decision to invest. 61 per cent of firms believed that the provision of roads was getting worse.[49]

In the late 1990s, infrastructure investment in the UK as a proportion of GDP was only 1.39 per cent compared to an OECD average of 3.14 per cent. It had increased to 1.77 per cent of GDP by 2004, but still badly lagged behind the OECD average of 3.13 per cent. The think tank Policy Exchange recently compiled what it believed to be the minimum level of adequate investment in UK infrastructure – a colossal £434 billion in total, with £120 billion of investment needed in transport alone.[50]

In transport, our record of underinvestment has left the country with a railway optimised for Victorian times. Our motorway network has barely been updated since its construction forty years ago. Only 30 per cent of UK railways are electrified, compared to more than 70 per cent in Belgium, Sweden and the Netherlands. China has already constructed a motorway network ten times the size of the UK's, and the UK has a shorter road length per person than any other major country. Spain, France and Germany each have motorway networks more than twice the size of the UK's.[51]

In order to remain competitive, we will need to upgrade near all our transport networks. We will need more roads, and further experimentation in managing demand through new systems of road pricing. Our

---

48   Going for Growth, OECD, 2010, pg 150
49   Helm, et al., 2009, pg 6
50   Helm, et al., 2009
51   Wellings, et al., 2008, pg 8

airports in the South East are already full. To meet demand in the coming thirty years, will need at least three new runways. Passenger numbers on our railways are booming, and demand can only be met through significant investment – preferably in a new high speed network.

While such investment in our transport sectors is badly needed, we will only be able to meet our challenging environmental targets by investing in our energy infrastructure at the same time. Electrifying our transport infrastructure will require much higher levels of energy generation. To move to a low carbon future, we will need a new generation of power generation, whether that be in the form of nuclear power or more renewable forms. As much as a third of our power generation capacity is soon to reach the end of its lifespan.[52] In order to meet EU targets, we need to generate 15 per cent of our energy from renewable sources by 2020.

Alongside globalisation, the most obvious trend in the new economy is the rise and rise of the internet. The UK is well placed to take advantage of this trend through its language, time zone and specialities in computing and the creative industries. In order to fully take advantage of the benefits, the country will need to invest in upgraded communication networks, both in broadband and mobile networks.

In order to pay for this investment, the country will need to look at new forms of financing. The record of traditional direct government investment is not encouraging, but there are significant opportunities to expand private-public financing. The government should look into making it easier for the public, individual investors

---

52   Helm, et al., 2009, pg 24

and pension funds savings to put money into infrastructure projects; perhaps through giving favourable tax treatment to bonds. Creating a more consistent approach to long term investment will reduce the risks for investors and, in turn, lower the costs of borrowing.

While national and London-based investments often get the most media attention, it is also important that the market works to ensure investment where it is needed across the country. Again, rather than try to manage this from the centre, we will almost certainly see better results by increasing localism. While there are risks, giving councils the power to raise their own bonds or borrowing would stop the Treasury from being the ultimate arbiter for all public investment. The US has already seen significant success from what is known as Tax Increment Financing, in which local authorities can pay for new investment by borrowing part of what are predicted to be the future tax revenues. The UK is now starting to investigate this model, with the first project likely to be a southerly extension of the Northern Line.

The challenge for future governments will be ensuring that the economy receives the investment it needs, while simultaneously not wasting money on white elephants or grand projets. This will not be easy.

Standing up for the hard-working majority

The summer of 2011 was marked by a ripple of industrial unrest across Britain. On 30 June, thousands of teachers walked out in England and Wales, joined by civil servants, including border officials, coastguard controllers, 999 operators and jobcentre staff. Elsewhere, London commuters narrowly avoided tube strikes, while binmen in Southampton let the rubbish pile up, and further votes for strikes by council workers took place in Birmingham and Doncaster. With 25 million workers in the private sector and 5 million in the public sector, the strikes threw light on the emergence of a 20/80 economy that has arisen in Britain over the past decade. Twenty per cent enjoy above average pay and gold-plated pensions, subsidised by the 80 per cent for whom no such benefits exist. In reality, most public sector workers also recognise – even if they do not like – the case for change.

The summer strikes shared a common feature. For all the hubris and hype from union leaders, not one of the four striking unions could muster the support of a majority of their members. Just 23 per cent of the Universities and Colleges Union (UCU), 29 per cent of the Association of Teachers and Lecturers (ATL) and 37 per cent of the National Union of Teachers (NUT) voted to strike. Strike action by the Public and Commercial Services Union (PCSU) was backed by a mere 20 per cent of those balloted. Bob Crow had a mandate from a mere 379 tube drivers – 29 per cent of his members – to blackmail Londoners with the threat of strikes by his Rail, Maritime and Transport union (RMT). In Southampton, Birmingham and Doncaster, Unite and Unison achieved 21–22 per cent support for strikes. In short, most public sector union members did not stand behind their leaders' posturing.

Union bosses spoke of the forthcoming disruption with ill-disguised delight – the opening shot in a battle between unions and the Con-Dem government. Unison's General Secretary, Dave Prentis, conjured the spectre of 'the biggest action since 1926', the year of the General Strike. Paul Kenny, the General Secretary of the GMB union, threatened David Cameron and Nick Clegg with 'the biggest civil disobedience campaign your tiny little minds have dreamt of'. Not to be outdone, the RMT leadership warned of a campaign of 'national resistance' across the rail sector if the government tries to enact the recommendations of the McNulty review of the railways. This highlighted up to £1billion of savings without compromising services, including by cracking down on union-inspired Spanish practices. Unsurprisingly, the strikes on 30 June fell short of the rhetoric of their leaders. Most public sector employees chose not to strike and lose pay. Most schools stayed open, and just one in five civil servants went on strike.

The current complaints over pay and pensions pale when compared to the epic past struggles of the union movement. Chartists, early unions and social reformers pioneered great struggles against injustice. Heroes like Annie Besant fought to protect workers from carcinogenic phosphorous in the 1888 match girls' strike, while the East London dockers' strike a year later rallied against the mercenary exploitation of casual labour. Partly as a result of their own successes over many years – in working standards and employment law – trade union membership has slumped from a peak of over 13 million members in 1979 to just 6.7 million today. It is overwhelmingly concentrated in the public sector, where 56 per cent of employees are unionised. In the private sector, union membership has fallen to just 15 per cent.

Today's union bosses are a shadow of their predecessors. They still hanker for the ideological struggles of a bygone era, and yearn for the political confrontation that accompanied it. But the oppression and social inequity of that era has long since evaporated – a sign of progress, a hallmark of the unions' own success. Consequently, they now find themselves defending the indefensible.

Take the RMT union, which held four tube strikes in late 2010, with 33 per cent support. It did so to protest against plans to cut 800 staff, mainly from ticket offices. The rationale for change was clear: customers are increasingly buying tickets online or at self-service machines. London Underground's plan involved no compulsory redundancies and all stations would still be manned. Still, Bob Crow bellowed that these modest reforms would turn the tube into a 'death trap'.

This was not an isolated incident. The RMT previously threatened to strike on the Docklands Light Railway, because the operator wanted to add an extra carriage to trains, to ease overcrowding. The union said the extra work was unacceptable without a pay rise. Examples of these Spanish practices are widespread in the industry, including drivers demanding 45 minutes before a journey to get a train ready to depart – despite the fact that maintenance staff do most of the preparation, right up to putting the key in the ignition for the drivers.

The tube strikes threatened in summer 2011 were part of a campaign to reinstate a driver, Arwyn Thomas, fired for abusing a colleague working on a strike day in 2010. The ballots were organised while an employment tribunal was still considering its decision on the case. It subsequently found that the employee had been guilty of misconduct, but should not have been fired for it. Ironically, given that the unions campaigned for stronger employment laws over many years, Bob Crow refused to leave the tribunal to resolve the case, and sought to pre-empt its rulings. That may help explain why just 20 per cent of Mr Thomas's fellow union members backed the strike ballot on the Northern line where he worked.

The RMT may be the worst offender – but it is not the only one. The teaching unions and the PCSU launched their coordinated strike in June to fight changes to public sector pensions. They did so despite the glaring imbalance between what is on offer to public and private sector workers. Currently, public sector workers earn more (£473/week, as opposed to £455/week), retire earlier (at 55 or 60, as opposed to 65) and enjoy better pensions than their private sector equivalents. The Institute for Fiscal Studies has estimated that the average difference between public and private sector pay and pensions amounts to 12 per cent of earnings. Policy Exchange calculates that this gap may be as wide as 43 per cent on an hourly basis.

This situation is patently unfair, but the coalition has striven to ensure that the impact of its reforms is fair to the public sector. Reformed public sector pensions would still deliver career average income on retirement, well beyond the reach of most private sector employees, while those on the lowest incomes will receive further protection. Equally, the public sector pay freeze does not apply to those earning £21,000 or less – a cushion that will not protect workers in businesses or charities up and down the country.

Union intransigence to any change is unsustainable at a time when record government debt and changing demographics are imposing huge strains on the general taxpayer. Life expectancy at 65 is now rising by a year every four years. Of current pensioners, 1 in 9 women, and 1 in 14 men, will reach their 100th birthday. Rather than acknowledge this and work towards a solution, Mark Serwotka, General Secretary of the PCSU, branded the government's response to ex-Labour minister, Lord Hutton's, recommendations for reform 'a highly political attack on the public sector'.

Union leaders are woefully out of touch with the economic realities facing the country. Those who call for zero cuts and no restraint in public sector pensions and pay risk alienating the hard-working majority, who have felt the pinch during a recession that saw the UK economy contract by 6 per cent.

Union bosses are also increasingly disconnected from the priorities of their own members. 86 per cent of strikes in 2010 were in the public sector, but in a recent survey by the Chartered Institute for Personnel and Development, 54 per cent of public sector workers said they were not willing to lose pay by going on strike. Declining union membership may partly reflect the frustration this detachment causes; RMT membership among tube drivers has fallen by 27 per cent since 2008.

There is wider evidence that union bosses are out of touch with their membership. Len McCluskey, the rabble-rousing boss of Unite, was elected by a paltry 7 per cent of its 1.4 million members. Bob Crow, a former member of the Communist Party, earns £145,000 a year, but lives in a housing association home intended for low-paid workers.

More generally, when strikes are called with minority support, the majority are often corralled and pressured into supporting them. RMT members are 'instructed' not to work on strike days. In 2008, Unison members were told that they were 'expected to abide by the decision of the majority' – in a strike backed by 15 per cent of their membership. In 2011, the University and College Union advised its members to 'target' non-striking staff at the picket line, despite less than a quarter of them having voted to strike. In June 2011, the NUT wrote to schools suggesting they would be liable under health and safety law if they opened during strikes. This concerted pressure and coercion is applied whether or not members voted for strike action. There are now thirty-seven union leaders taking home six figure salaries, insulated from the impact that striking has on many workers, who can ill afford to forfeit wages for the sake of bombastic but hollow declarations of class warfare and revolution.

The general public can only watch with rising frustration. An ICM poll in March 2011 found that 57 per cent of voters back the current pace of deficit reduction, or think cuts should go further. Public opinion is particularly hostile when public sector unions go on strike to protect practices which vanished in the private sector years ago. In June 2011, a ComRes poll found 63 per cent of voters thought that public sector workers wouldn't win sympathy for strike action, 'because everyone has to shoulder the burden of cuts'. The public rightly ask the question: how can bus drivers in Sheffield be striking for the right to retire at fifty (as happened in 2009), when the state pension age is rising to sixty-six?

The international comparison is equally worrying. In 2009, a comparatively quiet year for industrial action in this country, Britain lost 455,000 working days to strikes – compared to Germany which lost 64,000 working days, and the US which lost 124,000 working days.

Minority strikes are not a new phenomenon. They were held by the RMT in 2002 and 2009 – in each case causing massive disruption for commuters, and costing London's economy around £50 million each day. Bus drivers in Leeds and employees at the BBC have also gone on strike with substantially less than 50 per cent support. The PCSU led an earlier public sector walkout in February 2010 with only 20 per cent support.

The difference today is that a minority of militant union leaders are stepping up their efforts, having found a new political cause to rally around. Industrial action looks less like an effort to secure reasonable conditions for union members, and more like a nakedly political attempt to derail the coalition's efforts to cut the deficit and reform vital public services.

Even moderate union leaders despair. In advance of the strikes on 30 June, one anonymously told *The Guardian* that he feared the strikes would look 'half-hearted and weak ... ritualistic and tokenistic'. Yet, hardliners remain determined to take on the government. Unison's Dave Prentis declared, 'Every day we keep up the pressure, we wear them down, sap their strength and bring them closer to breaking point.' Britain cannot afford to reach that breaking point, and the hard-working majority – across the public and private sector – resent such brinkmanship in pursuit of unreasonable demands.

That is why strike law reform is long overdue. Currently, unions only need the support of a majority of those voting in the ballot to call industrial action. The abstention of those who decline to vote is taken as a tacit endorsement. A modest change would be to require a majority of support from union members before a strike can proceed – especially in the emergency services and transport sector, where scope for mass disruption to the public is so high. The unions reply that many politicians are not elected by a majority of their voters. But, no-one – least of all MPs – has the coercive legal power to paralyse vital infrastructure in this way. Union leaders have a unique power – and corresponding legal immunity from being sued – and it is not unreasonable to expect it to be exercised responsibly. It is wrong that a militant minority can blackmail the hard-working majority, with such a thin base of support from within the unions' own membership.

Proposals for a voting threshold have been backed by the Mayor of London, the CBI and Policy Exchange. On 12 January 2011, David Cameron told the House of Commons: 'I am very happy to look at this argument, because I do not want to see a wave of irresponsible strikes, not least when they are not supported by a majority of people taking part'. The public agree. A YouGov poll in June showed 59 per cent support for a threshold of 50 per cent or higher, to combat minority strikes.

Contrary to union protestations, this is not an especially high bar. A number of other EU countries already have such thresholds, including Denmark, the Czech Republic, Poland and Slovakia.

At the same time, the government should cut the tens of millions of taxpayers' money being used to pay for union organisers and activities across the public sector. If the unions can afford to pay their leaders up to £180,000 in salaries and benefits, and give millions in political donations to the Labour Party each year, why should the taxpayer be subsidising its core business – especially at a time when union leaders are fomenting strike action which hurts the public?

Finally, the balloting arrangements for strikes should be made more transparent. Ballot papers should also specify a particular grievance. Currently, some unions say nothing on the ballot paper about what a strike is about, but rather circulate a list of general grievances against the employer, wrapped up in general political propaganda. Ending this practice would ensure union members know the nature of the grievance they are voting on, and allow the employer to obtain an injunction against industrial action which is being pursued on the thin pretext of an earlier dispute. Ballots for strike action in the public sector should specify the relevant legal employer, as already happens in the private sector. The legal employer of most public sector workers is at a much lower level than that at which strike ballots are currently held. It is a particular hospital or university that employs most workers, not the system as a whole. This reform would prevent 'aggregated' ballots, which are regularly used to turn local trade disputes into a wave of nationwide strike action.

The irony is that orchestrated national pay bargaining by the unions has kept public sector pay suppressed, because the unions have fought performance-related pay tooth and nail. Take teaching, for example. The coalition is seeking to improve the status of teachers. Education Secretary, Michael Gove, has announced plans to reform teacher training, so students spend more time in the classroom, while the standing of the profession is being raised by requiring candidates to have at least a 2:2 degree to receive funding. Teachers will be better protected from malicious allegations by proposals to speed up investigations and protect their anonymity. Schools will also have more freedom to attract and reward outstanding staff, breaking the restrictions imposed by national pay deals. This is crucial to attracting the best and brightest graduates into the teaching profession. Yet, the teaching unions have opposed moves towards greater focus on individual performance. They know this would cut both ways, and expose some teachers' unacceptable under-performance. As of 2010, just eighteen teachers in this country have ever been struck off for incompetence over the last forty years. No-one wants to sack teachers gratuitously. But, the cosseting of under-performing teachers prevents enhanced remuneration for highly performing ones – precisely those we need to drive up educational standards.

Today, the role of a vocal minority of militant union bosses undermines the legacy of a union movement that struggled heroically against palpable injustices and for decent working conditions. This hard-line minority of union leaders, often with inflated salaries, is pursuing a militant political agenda which is disconnected from reality, rather than engaging in a reasonable dialogue with public sector employers and the government. The union leaders increasingly resemble the entrenched vested interests which they used to oppose. Strike law reform offers the opportunity to re-focus union leaders on the priorities of their members, while protecting the wider public from chaos and economic damage. The government must demonstrate its resolve in order to ensure that a militant minority is not given free rein to hold the hard working majority to ransom.

The brain drain is the greatest threat to British prosperity

Today, with the internet, working and living abroad is a very real choice for millions of people in this country – as elsewhere. It marks a historic moment for the citizen's relationship with his country and government. Globalisation has changed the rules of the game. In the twentieth century, British governments of all political colours asked: what is the fair way to treat members of our society? In the twenty-first century, they will increasingly be forced to focus on a less insular and more outward-looking challenge: how to retain the most talented?

Governments have long since cherry-picked policies from countries around the world. The Conservative Party went into the 2010 election promising zero-tolerance police reform inspired by New York, welfare reform tried and tested in Wisconsin, schools policy based on a

Swedish model, a deficit reduction plan borrowed from Canada and immigration policy designed in Australia. If governments can pick and choose in a globalised world, why not their citizens?

In reality, they already are. The number of people leaving Britain each year has risen by a third since 1997, while the number of Brits departing for foreign countries rose by two-thirds between 1998 and 2006, when recession temporarily stemmed the tide. A thousand people leave Britain each day. The largest category is those between twenty-five and forty-four years old – and most are going to take up, or in search of work. There are now more British graduates living abroad than from any other country in the OECD – more than the US and Germany combined, despite their larger populations. Where are they going? While some are moving to southern Europe (often to retire), the majority head where the economic opportunities are greatest – including Australia, New Zealand, the US, Hong Kong and Canada. Why are they going? The individual reasons will often be very personal, but a YouGov poll in 2010 among financial service professionals found that the top four reasons for leaving the UK were: cost of living, quality of life, economic prospects and high taxes.

The level of tax has risen sharply, particularly on those creating the most wealth – the top 5 per cent of earners now pay almost half the income tax. But taxes have also gone up on the lowest incomes – the share of tax paid by the bottom quartile rose by a third between 2007 and 2009. Meanwhile, Britain's dependency culture has been fuelled by a welfare system that penalises those who want to take up a job. If you want to set up a business, the effective rate of corporation tax is eleventh highest in Britain, according to a recent survey of eighty-three countries. At every level, the tax system stifles ambition, enterprise and aspiration.

Unsurprisingly, Britain has slumped on the international economic rankings – from third to thirteenth on the World Economic Forum rankings for economic competitiveness, and from fifth to sixteenth on the Index of Economic Freedom. However, the longer-term risk is not just that Britain is a less attractive place for businesses to come. It is also increasingly a less attractive place for the best and brightest to stay. If the symptoms of economic malaise are clear for our generation, they are still more bleak for the next. By 2010, according to the National Institute for Economic and Social Research (NIESR), Britain had total public sector liabilities of £3.8 trillion – or four times the national debt after the Second World War. The NIESR reckons this equates to a tax bill of £200,000 on each member of the next generation just to enjoy the same level of public services we enjoy today. Would you hang around for that?

History offers two lessons for today's policy-makers. First, just as nations that rewarded innovation, enterprise, talent and hard-work prospered in the nineteenth and twentieth centuries, those that fail will stagnate – partly as a result of the brain drain. The opportunities for entrepreneurs, professionals and skilled workers to choose their government, country and way of life – á la carte from an increasingly international menu – will force competition, among governments, on a scale never seen before. Domestic politics may come to look less like a contest between mainstream parties, and more like a bidding war for global talent.

Second, while Europe's nationalistic rivalries led to two savage wars, competition was also one of the vital ingredients that drove Western civilisation. With the economies of Europe increasingly interwoven by trade and commerce, the risk of war on the continent has dramatically receded. However, the drive towards European economic, social and political integration is closing down the room for innovation and competition at national and regional levels. Where diverse, pluralistic and innovative Europe once led the world, an increasingly homogenous and monolithic Europe, governed by strait jacket laws is likely to fall behind. If competition made Europe great, integration has blunted its competitive edge.

In today's increasingly competitive world, there is no room for complacency. Countries around the world are absorbing the lessons from the Industrial Revolution that Britain seems to have forgotten. It is no surprise that many of our best and brightest are leaving the country. The media attention on the economy is distracted by the short term fluctuations of the economic cycle. In the long run however, the real mission of modern Conservatism must be to re-energise today's corporatist, over regulated and over taxed economy.

SUMMARY AGENDA

- Our tax system should be simplified and reformed, taxing consumption and pollution rather than savings and hard work.
- We should seek new funding for vital infrastructure, such as new transport, energy and communications networks. At the same time, we should reform planning laws to make it easier for businesses to grow the economy.
- We should reform union laws to require a majority of support from union members before a strike can proceed.

4. Environment: A Conservative Response to Climate Change

Few issues are spoken of in such apocalyptic tones as the threat of climate change. If we cannot tackle our current addiction to carbon, it is claimed, our civilisation itself may be at threat. We risk melted ice caps, devastated ecosystems, flooded countries and millions of new refugees.

The science is not yet exactly clear on the extent of the risks from climate change. It is still difficult to weigh up the balance between the small risk of a truly catastrophic outcome versus the certain harm of holding back economic growth. Nevertheless, the science is clear enough that the risk is worth taking seriously. In order to tackle such a challenge, we will need our very best technology, science, economics and policy making.

In other words, what is needed is a pragmatic response. Unfortunately, many activists are instead using the threat as an excuse simply to implement old agendas. Strident claims are made that the threat of climate change means that the government can no longer afford to maintain such a loose grip of the economy. Instead, it is argued, highly trained government planners must take a firmer hand, regulating our industries and daily lives. Some believe that the age of economic abundance is over – we will have to get used to rationing.

Take the case of transport: the threat of global warming, the environmentalists argue, means that we have to move from the road to public transport. Aviation has become an unaffordable luxury; we must halt its growth and optimise what capacity we already have. We have to place strict limits on the numbers of cars on our roads or planes flying from our airports.

This campaign of persuasion has been highly successful. Governments of all political persuasions have largely given up on road building. It is now government policy that no new runways should be built in the South East of England, even though demand is expected to double in the next thirty years.[53]

Already this is beginning to have effects on our international competitiveness. In the era of globalisation, trade and transport links are crucial for our continuing prosperity. We cannot expect to gain more trade with China if our businessmen do not have a regular service flying to places like Guangzhou. While other world cities such as Dubai plan six runway airports, Britain's Heathrow tries to struggle by with only two.

Beyond the economic impact, it is worth thinking of the social justice of such restrictions. The arrival of aviation brought international travel to the middle classes, but it remains a rare luxury for the working class. The poorest are more likely to holiday by the beach, while the rich enjoy ski trips or the summer house in France. More than 50 per cent of those with incomes below £20,000 didn't fly at all in the past year. By contrast, 50 per cent of those with incomes of £31,000 took two flights or more.

---

53   The Future of Air Transport White Paper, 2003

If we never build any more airports or runways, then aviation will only ever be affordable by the very rich.

Government planning has never been very good at the kind of innovation we would need to wean transport off fossil fuels. Indeed, we can see the costs of government planning by looking at the history of progress in transport. The government largely nationalised the sector at the end of the Second World War and, ever since, progress has more or less stalled. For the last fifty years, the shape of our transport systems has remained the same. The rocket age appears to have been a dead end. We still drive more or less the same type of cars. The first High Speed Rail appeared in 1964 in Tokyo, but the technology has spread only slowly. Our planes haven't noticeably moved on from the Boeing 747, first introduced in 1970.

To tackle climate change in transport and across our economy, the last thing we need is more planning. By endless restrictions, taxes and regulations we will simply make daily life more expensive for ordinary consumers, and make it harder for our companies to innovate. At the same time any limitations to our own carbon emissions will soon be outweighed by rapidly growing Asian economies.

Fundamentally the task of rationing the supply of carbon is no different from the task of rationing the supply of food. Markets automatically make the millions of micro decisions that effective rationing needs, giving each of us a say of what to do with a limited resource. They allow innovation to happen, and reward those who try out new ideas.

If we really want to lower our carbon emissions, we will almost certain need a thousand new innovations, fundamentally changing the supply chains throughout our economy. No politician or bureaucrat can hope to predict all this.

As economists have long argued, the best means of tackling climate change is through the creation of a carbon tax.[54] Such a tax would meet our climate obligations, while neither relying on the wisdom of bureaucrats nor adding unduly to regulation. A new carbon tax would allow us to do away with the umpteen complex environmental regulations and taxes that have been created over the last decades. Governments could stop trying to plan the future development of our energy and transport markets.

Part of the solution to climate change will almost certainly involve the further development of nuclear power. It is the only realistic way to cater for the UK's future energy demands and the lifestyle to which its citizens have grown accustomed. Britain's Kyoto target for cutting CO_2 emissions by 2012 was set at 12.5 per cent. France, which already derives 80 per cent of its electricity from nuclear power, has no Kyoto target at all.

A focus on nuclear requires political courage in the wake of the Fukishima Dai-ichi meltdown. But, as the last government's Chief Scientific Adviser, Sir David King, recently argued, 'nuclear power is even safer than we thought ... by far the safest method of power generation per amount of electricity produced: it provides relatively low-cost energy with a high level of safety'. It will necessitate some up-front investment from energy investors, and that will be reflected in energy bills in the short term. However, it remains the only credible medium term answer to our energy needs and environmental ambitions.

---

54 Alternatively we could use an emissions trading scheme, although there are political reasons to believe that this might be difficult.

Any future Conservative administration should certainly not ignore the potential threats from carbon change. We should be a world leader in negotiations for the implementation of an international carbon tax. However, introducing such a tax in one country alone is little more than gesture politics. Any additional restraint in Britain would be fast outweighed by the rapid development of Asia. Moreover, simply exporting our own carbon-intensive industries to China does little for the world's climate as a whole.

But while we should be advocates for increased environmentalism, we should be so in a way that is consistent with our liberal, conservative values. We know that the best way to seek innovation is not through more government plans. If we need to lower pollution, we should investigate more taxes – we should not put the whole of the economy under the control of bureaucrats.

Already, according to the Department for Transport, aviation pays £100 million more than the costs of both its carbon emissions and local pollution. Indeed, the UK already charges a very high tax level on petrol, making up around two-thirds of its cost – and meaning that prices are near double those experienced in the US.[55] There is little economic or environmental rationale to today's regulation holding back the growth of transport.

The government should not be in the business of limiting airports, or trying to persuade people out of their cars. It is not the government's place to ration our foreign holidays, or to create new energy technologies on its own. The government should apply whatever taxes are needed, and then let individuals take responsibility for their own decisions.

---

55   http://www.economist.com/blogs/freeexchange/2011/02/
     energy_prices

SUMMARY AGENDA

- We should use market mechanisms such as a Carbon Tax to tackle the challenge of climate change, rather than increased government planning and bureaucracy.
- We should have a strong plan to upgrade our roads and airports.

5. Welfare: Ending the 'Hand Out' Culture

When New Labour first arrived in power in May 1997, it could not have asked for a better economic inheritance. The combination of the previous administration's reforms and the worldwide 'Great Moderation', had granted Britain an economy with low interest rates, falling debt, and strong growth. Never would there a better opportunity to tackle the problems of long term youth unemployment and workers dumped on incapacity benefit.

Sure enough, before the 2007 financial crash brought the good times to an end, the British economy succeeded in adding millions of jobs over the decade of New Labour's rule. The economy as a whole grew at a rate of 2.5 per cent a year, leading some optimistic commentators to speculate that we had even moved to a permanently higher rate of growth.[56]

A problem was that the vast majority of these jobs did not go to British workers. Of the 1.67 million new

---

56   Diggle, et al., 2010

jobs created between 1997 and 2010, 99 per cent went to foreign-born workers.[57]

That is not to say that immigrants 'stole' those jobs, or that we should follow a Gordon Brown style policy of 'British Jobs for British Workers'. All the economic evidence shows immigration having next to no effect on native wages or living conditions.[58] Immigrants create as many jobs as they take. What it does show is that while new jobs were there for the taking in the British economy, British workers did not seem to want them.

Over a quarter of working-age adults in the UK now do not work.[59] There are now nearly 5 million working age people on benefits. Spending on benefits and tax credits has risen in real terms from £63 billion when New Labour came to power in 1997 to £87 billion in 2010. In the last ten years 1.4 million people have been on benefits for nine years or more, and almost 2 million children now grow up in households where nobody works at all.[60]

While the radical plans of Labour MP Frank Field were vetoed by the then Chancellor, the New Labour government did not entirely ignore the problem of long term unemployment. Its chosen policy instrument was a programme known as the New Deal, launched in 1998. By providing training and subsidised employment the New Deal aimed to give the unemployed the skills they'd need to prosper in the jobs market. The majority of the

---

57   http://www.spectator.co.uk/coffeehouse/5895033/british-jobs-for-british-workers.thtml

58   Kerr, et al., 2011

59   Department for Work and Pensions, 2010, pg 9

60   Department for Work and Pensions, 2010, pg 4

funding was earmarked for the New Deal for Young People programme, aimed specifically at what is known in the jargon as NEETs: Not in Education, Employment or Training.

The New Deal did not work. Despite spending over £2 billion on the New Deal, nearly 1 million young people aged 16–25 are now classed as NEETs. In 1997, 18.8 per cent of young people were NEETs; in 2006, 18.9 per cent were, almost no progress in nine years.[61] Youth unemployment actually fell at a slower rate after the New Deal was introduced than before. The cost of every job created was over £22,000 and in any case only 40 per cent of New Deal leavers entered long term unsubsidised jobs.[62]

Activists from the Left sometimes like to claim that the primary reasons people are unemployed are insufficient training or a lack of demand in the wider economy. The failure of the New Deal in a benign economic environment shows that it isn't this simple.

As industries change and evolve, workers may lose their jobs and have to shift careers. In the modern world, we are increasingly expected to undertake multiple careers. There are considerably fewer 'jobs for life'.

But if we want to sustain our dynamic economy, we need to make sure that some workers don't get left behind.

It now seems clear that neither training nor boosting the wider economy will in themselves be sufficient. What is needed is a more conservative revolution: giving individuals the confidence, the initiative and the responsibility to seek out their own work.

---

61   Centre for Social Justice, 2009, pg 2
62   Bogdanor, 2004, pg 8

The problems with welfare

The task of looking after the poor and vulnerable has always been divided between the private and public sectors. Welfare systems are not just about looking after the unemployed, but also the young, the elderly and those suffering from ill health. Perhaps the original and still strongest form of the welfare state is the family. Where the family could not provide, individuals have instead looked to private bodies such as friendly societies, guilds or insurance policies to look after them in case of misfortune. As families and society have lost relative importance as sources of mutual insurance, government has increasingly stepped in in their place.

The first complete codified Poor Law was introduced in Elizabethan times in 1597. Throughout the centuries the relative generosity or harshness of the assistance given to the poor has fluctuated. The New Poor Law of 1834 centralised the system and set up the regime of workhouses. In 1908 a pension was introduced for the over 70s, and in 1911 a system of compulsory national insurance was created. In 1921, the system was extended to cover those who hadn't yet contributed themselves. The system was fundamentally reformed again under Beveridge in 1945, and the range of benefits and number of people covered vastly expanded.

While government benefits from extensive resources, it suffers from being far removed from the lives of those it would help. The more removed the giver is from the needy, the harder it is to properly get the balance right between the two central missions of welfare: relieving poverty, and supporting fairness. The more we support the poor, the harder is to remain fair to those who have remained in work. The problem with unfairness is not just a moral one. In the long run an unfair system encourages more people out of work permanently.

Both 'fairness' and 'poverty' are contested terms. Those of different political persuasions can argue at length whether the fairness we need should be a more meritocratic society, or simply a more equal distribution of resources. Similarly, we can conceive of poverty as absolute shortage of food and shelter, or in terms of being cut off from the mainstream in society.

There is no perfect answer to such philosophical questions. Most people's beliefs about poverty and fairness lie somewhere in the middle of the extreme views of the ideologues. What seems clear is that we won't ever achieve perfect 'fairness' or do away with 'poverty' simply by increasing benefits. We should aim to give people the skills they need to enjoy and improve their own lives, rather than remain permanently tethered to the benefits office. Giving the poor an extra ten pounds a week will not by itself bring about change. Giving them the confidence and guidance to take on a new job will.

Our current benefits system still largely takes the form envisioned by Beveridge. Yet the Beveridge report was published in 1944, nearly seventy years ago. It is clear that we have failed to create a system that does not, as he desired, 'stifle incentive, opportunity or responsibility'. We have done something to tackle four of his 'Giant Evils' in Want, Disease, Ignorance, and Squalor, yet we do not seem to be doing as well at tackling the last: Idleness.

There are two fundamental problems with the welfare state, or, as it sometimes known, social insurance. While governments have marketed the system as nothing more than a compulsory insurance scheme, this has been little more than an accounting fiction. Rather than save its citizens' wealth as a pension company, the government has always paid recipients from the direct funds of current taxpayers. When the country's population was growing and largely young, this allowed for recipients to receive far more generous benefits than they had paid in. Now that the population is aging it means that the system is becoming rapidly unaffordable. Social insurance is always more susceptible than private insurance to raids by short sighted governments.

But the main problem is that the system currently fails in striking a balance between supporting the poor and making sure there are also incentives to work. The welfare system today still fails to pay recipients the benefits they are due, and to encourage people effectively to get work. Too remote from the people it is supposed to support, the system tries to make up for its lack of personal connection with increasingly complex rules.

But the complexity of these rules creates its own problems. The DWP's benefit rules take up an entire fourteen volumes, in total 8,690 pages. There are a further four volumes and 1,200 pages on Housing Benefit and Council Tax. [63] Administering the system costs the DWP £2 billion a year, HM Revenues & Customs £500 million and local authorities a further £1 billion. The complexity induces chronic error and fraud, costing the taxpayer over £5 billion a year – £2.1 billion in tax credits and £3.1 billion in benefits. [64] The complexity also makes it hard for customers to know what they are entitled to. Working Tax Credit has a take up of just 57 per cent of those eligible. Customers are underpaid

---

63   Martin, 2009
64   Martin, 2009, pg 11

by £1.3 billion a year in benefits and £260 million in tax credits. [65]

The many benefits, taxes and allowances the government administers all interact in increasingly unpredictable ways. It is difficult for HMRC to work out the financial implications of any change in life circumstances, let alone for individuals to do the calculations themselves. It must be hard for individuals to take responsibility for their own decisions when they do not even know what their options are.

As bad as its complexity are the poor incentives the system creates. The withdrawal of benefits when a claimant takes a new job means that they in effect face a second income tax. According to the DWP, over 100,000 people face a marginal rate of 90 per cent. Just under two million people face a marginal rate of over 60 per cent.[66]

The impressions of claimants are even worse than the reality. When polled for the think tank Centre for Social Justice, only 25 per cent of claimants thought they would be better off from working. 39 per cent thought they would be worse off. [67]

It is difficult to summon up the motivation to search for a hard job when one can earn the same amount on benefits. In order to make more people want to take a job, we will have to do a better job at ensuring that work always pays.

Of course, money isn't everything. The incentives that keep people trapped on benefits aren't all financial. In order to bring people back into the real economy, we need to help build their self-respect and responsibility, as

---

65 Department for Work and Pensions, 2010, pg 8

66 Department for Work and Pensions, 2010, pg 11

67 Centre for Social Justice, 2009, pg 7

well as simply reintroducing the habit of going to work. From an earlier age we need to instil more of an entrepreneurial spirit. The hard working, initiative taking immigrants have not found it impossible to find work when they need it. Our current school system is not good at teaching entrepreneurialism or giving individuals responsibility for themselves.

There is rarely a week in Parliament without a financial education event or an exhortation that more must be done to educate school pupils about how to use their money wisely. However we send mixed messages. Somehow it is believed to be the State's responsibility to ensure young people are on the housing ladder or that the vulnerable are not saddled with debt. The danger is that this leads to a lack of responsibility.

That is not to say that the difficulty in obtaining work is entirely the individual's fault. To make it easier to create jobs, we need to free up the economy as a whole. New regulations and restrictions on wages such as the Minimum Wage make it harder to offer entry level positions. We need to be very careful to make sure we don't make matters more difficult with further ill thought through legislation, for example hasty bans on internships and training positions.

Further, we need to make it easier for families to move across the country to find work. In a changing economy, some parts of the country sometimes decline while others boom. In the nineteenth century, workers in their millions moved from the country to the industrial towns of the North. Now, workers may have to move from other declining areas in search of jobs.

But moving in the UK is not easy. Housing is expensive, and difficult to find. Aside from making it hard to obtain a new home, this also makes it difficult to leave the old one. The high levels of housing benefit needed to allow workers to live in central London mean few will want to move away and give up their benefit.

Part of the route to a more dynamic economy is freeing up the housing market. Ultimately, the only long term way to do that is through easing up planning regulation and liberating Britain's social housing, subjects discussed elsewhere.

Welfare reform

The coalition government has taken bold steps to improve welfare. The most crucial element of the coalition's plans is a benefit known as the Universal Credit. The current complex welfare system is to be integrated and simplified. In the future every claimant who takes on work shall earn at least an extra 55 per cent of their new wages. There will always be some motivation in the future to take on work and start your way on the career ladder.

While these reforms are a good start, they are unlikely to provide enough motivation to move every claimant into a job. The reforms are expected to bring 300,000 households into work, leaving 3.6 million households still workless.[68] There is a danger that they will encourage some workers into simply taking up part time work.

As well as improving incentives, we need to improve the fairness of the reforms. The coalition has made some progress in this regard, but we could go still further in reforming welfare to better shape the motivations of its participants.

The lodestar of welfare reform advocates across the world is the bi-partisan Wisconsin reforms crafted in 1990s America. The Wisconsin reforms were based on

---

68   Oakley, et al., 2011

two key principles: claimants had to work as well as simply undergo training, and social security offices had to compete with private sector companies. These reforms succeeded in dropping the welfare rolls by 94 per cent; they cut child poverty by 20 per cent and the cost of welfare by half. [69]

Britain must learn from Wisconsin and integrate more of what is known as 'conditionality' into Britain's welfare system. Benefits should be conditional on claimants making a genuine effort on their own to seek out work. The crucial difference between Wisconsin and Labour's New Deal, was that the New Deal allowed its participants to choose training over work experience. While training can be important, it fails to give the claimant as good a motivation to seek their own job.

At the moment the main conditionality in the British system is that claimants on Job Seekers Allowance are supposed to provide evidence of at least three 'job-related activities' each week. It is not clear that this system is either strict enough or being sufficiently monitored. People already in work of course wish to support the unemployed, but their sympathy evaporates when they learn that claimants spend on average only 8 minutes a day looking for a job.[70] When polled, half of the respondents believed that that the unemployed should be spending at least three hours a day looking for new work.[71] Nearly 70 per cent agreed that jobseekers should lose their benefits if they turn down excessive job offers.[72]

---

69   Bogdanor, 2004, pg 9
70   Oakley, et al., 2011
71   Oakley, et al., 2011, pg 4
72   Oakley, et al., 2011, pg 7

There is also a case for looking again at time limits. In Britain, the amount claimants are paid in benefits stays practically the same no matter how long the person has been out of work. In the US, federal unemployment insurance ends after half a year. It seems clear that this increases the incentives to look for work. In several European countries where similar time limits exist, evidence shows that claimants are 80 per cent more likely to find a job in the week before their benefits run out.[73]

Another avenue to explore is the idea of workfare. Rather than obtain their benefits for nothing, the unemployed should be expected to contribute something back, undertaking unpaid or low paid work. Not only does this strike many as more fair but it helps to build the habits of discipline and self-responsibility that are so necessary in the search for a long term career.

The exact pattern of reforms will need further experimentation. Indeed, there is a good case for allowing private profit and non-profit bodies to experiment with their own benefit structures and rules. Devolving responsibility will allow professionals to use more of their own judgement. Experimenting with greater conditionality is clearly a sensitive matter, but handled responsibly it can help give the poor the support they need.

In the long term, we could require people to insure themselves against unemployment to a reasonable level. Then we could have a lower 'hardship level' to be administered on a local basis for those with no insurance. This would mean judgement and local knowledge can be used about whether an individual is capable of working rather than relying on a central edict.

---

73   Triggs, et al., 2010, pg 13

In short, the current government's reforms are a good start, taking away the worst distortions of the current benefits system. However, we will need both carrot and stick, tax incentives and conditionality, if we are to truly make our economy a dynamic one in which anyone can retrain and embark on multiple careers.

It is important to remember that the goal of such reforms is not simply to cut back on the UK's benefits bill, important as that may be in difficult fiscal circumstances. The real priority is to help people escape the poverty trap and move to a life of dignity, purpose and fulfilment. Some believe that the best way to help the poor is by continually increasing their benefits – but we can and should be far more ambitious than that.

Social Housing

It would be overly simplistic to claim that badly structured benefits were responsible for the poverty in British society. Indeed, if we are to understand the origins of deprivation in society, we cannot simply consider educational failure, health inequality or benefit dependence in isolation. Often there is a high correlation between all three, largely dependent on where someone lives. If we are to address many of the current social problems in society, we must confront what we might consider the 'politics of place'. High levels of deprivation are often concentrated in a single street, even a single postcode.

In recent years, much has been done to expose the dramatic inequalities that continue to exist within society. More detailed geographical data such as the creation of 32,482 Lower Super Output Areas (LSOAs) has been able to reveal appallingly low levels of educational attainment or life expectancy in tiny pockets of disadvantage. For example, in 631 LSOAs, 10 per cent or fewer go onto higher education; in 362 LSOAs, that figure is actually 1 per cent or below. In contrast, there are 1401 LSOAs in which 90 per cent or more pupils go onto university. When it comes to staying in education post-sixteen, there are 3,084 LSOAs where no pupil stays on beyond sixteen, and 15,319 where 25 per cent or fewer decide to stay on.

No doubt as our data improves, a more definite picture will emerge. Yet it is clear, that areas of social housing remain a persistent contributor to the levels of deprivation in society, whether that be bad health, educational failure or a collapse into chronic welfare dependency.

The figures tell the story of the past twenty years well enough. Of those living in social housing in 2004, 82 per cent had also been social housing tenants ten years before. Inhabitants of social housing have become relatively poorer, as poverty has become concentrated in these areas. In 1981, 47 per cent of social tenants were in employment; this has now fallen to 32 per cent. Full-time employment has fallen from 43 per cent to 22 per cent during the time period. The likelihood of someone living in social housing having both their neighbours on either side of them in full time work has fallen from just under one in two to one in nine.

Since its establishment, Right to Buy has allowed over 1.8 million social housing tenants to achieve their dream of owning their own property, and with it the chance of greater independence. Rightly, the policy has been heralded as one of the most innovative and important of the Thatcher government, breaking not only a cycle of dependency upon the State but creating a new constituency of voters for the Conservative Party. Yet we must admit that there are areas where this policy is unlikely to ever reach.

It is in large 'flatted' estate areas – where two-thirds of social housing is located – that Right to Buy has had little impact, with only 12 per cent of flats being sold under RTB. This is unsurprising since 60 per cent of social housing tenants in flats live on housing benefits.

And yet it is in these same areas that some of the nation's most desperate poverty is located. 40 per cent of all unemployment is concentrated in these areas. The situation is a desperate one, and one which will only continue to deteriorate if multiple forms of deprivation are allowed to cluster and concentrate. It is worrying that of the new entrants to the social rented sector (SRS) in 2003/4, only 26 per cent were in full-time work compared with 47 per cent in 1981.

At the same time, mobility throughout the social housing market has stagnated. Turnover has shrunk—turnover rates in the social rented sector are now below 10 per cent, with only 9 per cent of social renters having a tenure of residence of less than a year, compared to 38 per cent of private renters. This form of social housing mobility is crucial for freeing up supply so that many families can access the housing they desperately need. Already the number of people living in temporary accommodation, either in hostels or bedsits, has risen from 44,000 in 1997 to over 100,000 in 2005; nor is this situation 'temporary' – in London, 37 per cent of households in temporary accommodation had spent two or more years there; four times the rate in 2000. The latest figures reveal that 8 per cent of English households were on a housing waiting list.[74] Without radical action to transform mobility this situation will only worsen.

---

74   Katie Schmuecker, 'The good, the bad and the ugly – housing demand 2025' IPPR, 2011, pg 6

Over the last two decades, approximately 160,000 new dwellings have been added to the social housing stock in England. If this rate continues, there will be a projected shortfall of 750,000 by 2025.[75] Finding innovative new ways to use the existing social housing stock is essential to prevent demand for housing further outstripping supply.

We recognise that neither situation is sustainable. To address both, there needs to be a transformation in the way we view social housing. Social housing provision must be a hand up, rather than a hand down. And rather than being seen as a state of existence, social housing needs to be recognised as a journey towards home ownership, placing greater independence in the hands of individuals.

The key to achieving this is to generate mobility within the social housing sector itself. Crucial to improving the life chances of individuals living in social housing is to increase turnover in these existing dwellings. By increasing turnover, we will create far more opportunities for regenerating the social housing market than by simply building new social housing units alone.

There needs to be a revolution in the supply-side of social housing, in order for the current housing provision to be improved. Getting families off rising waiting lists will only take place once we have unblocked the stagnation that has set in.

This means looking at what we do with the existing supply of social housing.

Of the 4 million social rented units in 2005, more than 93 per cent were ten years old. As the Hills Report

---

75   Katie Schmuecker ,'The good, the bad and the ugly – housing demand 2025' IPPR, 2011, pg 1

on Social Housing provision observed, 'even if 40,000 new units were added each year for the next decade, we would already have nine-tenths of the social rented stock that we will have in 2016.' However, Right to Buy, stymied by increases in the value of discounts available for purchases is no longer able to have the same impact it once had: in 2009–2010, the Department for Communities and Local Government reports that there were just 3,100 Right to Buy sales in England.

It is time to renew the principle of Right to Buy with the new goal of 'Right to Own'.

The aspiration to own one's own home is at the heart of British society. Yet the divide between that aspiration and reality is sadly widening. While 95 per cent of Britons expect to own their own home in their lifetime, only 49 per cent of under 35s own property today compared to 59 per cent in 2001. As a result, it is estimated that 3.1 million of those currently under 35 will still remain in rented accommodation at the age of 65. At the same time as property prices are becoming more inaccessible to future generations, the number of households in England is now projected to increase from 20.9 million in 2003 to 25.7 million by 2026, an increase of 23 per cent or annual growth of 209,000.

Establishing a principle of Right to Own within our social housing sector could revolutionise this, unlocking the resources and capital tied up in social housing. Through an extension of property rights, not only is a greater sense of independence and well-being created. As the work of the Peruvian economist Hernando de Soto has shown, the benign effects of widening property rights extend deeply into the establishment of mortgage lending, and creating a market that reaches beyond property itself. De Soto concentrates his research on unlocking the assets of those living in poverty, to allow them the freedom to make use of existing capital. This was done predominantly by formalising informal property arrangements, which in turn encouraged credit and business lending. In *The Mystery of Capital*, De Soto calculated that there was $9.3 trillion of 'dead capital' in the developing world, an immeasurably valuable resource.

Clearly the situation in the UK is very different, with a well codified legal system of property ownership. However, by treating our stock of social and council housing as an untapped economic resource rather than merely bricks and mortar, we can break away from what still remains a statist model of council housing, towards a new emphasis on ownership and value.

There are around 4 million social homes in England,[76] with an estimated market value of around £250 billion.[77] Even freeing up just a tenth of this under the 'Right to Own' concept, would create £7 billion in deposits for tenants, and £17.5 billion in capital to build new affordable housing. This is money that comes not out of the taxpayer's pocket, but simply from making better use of the available resources.

There is also an element of behavioural economics involved. A carefully constructed 'Right to Own' system would create an incentive for occupiers to treat the property well, as well as eventually to step into ownership. This scheme would further extend the advantages of 'Right to Buy', while at the same time freeing up social housing

---

76   http://www.localis.org.uk/images/Localis%20Principles%20
       for%20Social%20Housing%20Reform%20WEB.pdf

77   http://www.redington.co.uk/Redington/media/PDFs/knowl-
       edge/Redington%20Events/Robin-Caven-Opportunities-in-
       Social-Housing.pdf

for a fraction of the overall cost. Clearly such a scheme would have to involve a number of safeguards and be closely linked to responsible behaviour on the part of tenants. We envisage the equity stake being virtual rather than a cash lump sum, which would be transferred to a shared HomeBuy scheme for example.

How might a Right to Own scheme work? The basic principle is clear: by granting a tenant an automatic share in the equity of the property— this might vary depending on the nature of deprivation within an estate and also length of tenure— the scheme would encourage the property to be sold on the market. The tenant would receive a portion of the equity which they could then transfer into a shared home buy scheme, or even a new property, thereby giving them an automatic foot on the housing ladder. The remainder of the sale might then be reinvested in building new social housing stock to meet demand. Everyone wins: not only would tenants get a foot on the property ladder, but it would also create an increased supply of social housing able to sustainably fund its own regeneration. At the same time, the Right to Own would finally allow a market to be created within some of our most trenchant flatted housing estates where Right to Buy schemes have failed to make an impact.

There can be no Conservative principle sounder than wider property ownership. At the same time, by liberating 'dead equity', we can offer a hand to the most deprived areas of our country. In this way, social housing becomes a stepping stone, not a dead end.

Employment, pensions and families
While the concerns of the unemployed and the deprived are rightly the first concern of politicians, all of us interact with the welfare system throughout our lives. Many

aspects of our benefit system simply no longer make sense in the modern economy. Welfare is a relationship between government and the individual; it should not make it harder for new businesses to start or create jobs. And while welfare should always be there as a fall back measure, it should not be a replacement for our natural responsibilities.

Employment benefit reform
It was right that when people had a 'job for life' and many were less well-educated that the employer had a greater duty of care towards employees. However now, when many employees work for longer, move in and out of different sectors, or work for themselves, this model is less effective. In fact it hampers flexibility in the marketplace and puts large burdens on small employers. It creates 'handcuffs', both for employers and employees who want to move on.

State benefits are still predicated on a shorter working life and a single employer, with sole traders and freelancers often disregarded. In fact, in a longer working life, a more flexible freelance model has a lot to recommend it, with the individual 'owning' their insurance, savings and benefits that they derive. We should support a general move to stop requiring employers to administer state benefits and penalties

At the same time, we need to see the development of a strong Conservative approach to provide new flexibility and opportunity for Britain's working families. Today two thirds of couples with children under sixteen both work, whereas one third are single earner families. Conservative policies need to cater for this diversity.

At present, businesses pay new mothers 90 per cent of their pay for the first six weeks of maternity leave and then the Statutory Maternity Pay of £129 per week or 90 per cent of their pay (whichever is lower) for the following 33 weeks. The business is then able to claim this back from the government. The average payment is around £5,000. It would be better if this amount were made a flat sum and paid directly from the government to the parent as a 'Baby Bonus', reducing bureaucracy and complication.

Mothers and fathers would then be given an entitlement to unpaid leave from their employer. As a net amount is paid to a couple, the potential fraud inherent in current proposals of mother and father both claiming maximum pay are avoided. Employers could of course top this up as they do at the moment, offering staff additional paid or unpaid leave.

This system would use similar processes and standards of proof as Maternity Allowance which is paid direct by government. This reduces the need for employers to monitor the system and it would reduce their compliance costs. There would still be a compulsory two weeks paid maternity leave as there is at present. This would be administered in the same way as paid holiday by the employer.

The availability of flexible, affordable, high quality childcare is a pressing concern for families and critical to the wider economy. According to the OECD, the UK has one of the most expensive childcare systems in the world, accounting for 25 per cent of average income in 2004, compared to 14 per cent in the EU24 and 16 per cent in the OECD. The growth of employment in the service sector has created new low-to-middle earning jobs and presented parents with new challenges in meeting work and family commitments. The childcare market has failed to keep pace with changes in the nature of employment and the growth of dual earning and lone parent households. It is currently inadequate to meet the needs of families on low-to-middle incomes.

Much of the current debate suggests that there needs to be more subsidy of childcare. The problem is that there is restricted supply in a heavily regulated market place. Childcare providers are regulated by Ofsted in a three month process. In the last ten years childcare costs have risen steadily beyond inflation, even though more state places have been added to the market. The government provides universal free childcare for fifteen hours a week for those between three and four years old, as well as offering similar services to the most disadvantaged two year olds. However in 2006 the ability of parents to pay 'top-up' fees to state funded nurseries was removed, leading to private sector providers leaving the market. As Kate Peach, managing director of Early Years Childcare, stated 'if nurseries opt out or go out of business, disadvantaged children will lose access to high-quality settings and only the very wealthy will have access to high-quality childcare.' The ability to top up should be restored to enable more flexible supply in the market.

Social and long-term care

We must recognise that perhaps one of the biggest impending challenges that the UK faces is the challenge of an ageing population. This will put immense pressure on our budgets. The recent Dilnot Commission's report into long-term care has begun the debate about contribution and insurance mechanisms to help pay for care. Yet social care and care of the elderly has always remained outside of any discussions around the welfare state because Beveridge did not envisage people living much beyond a decade after retirement. As a result, the welfare state designed in the mid twentieth century will soon collapse under the weight of twenty-first century demands.

The challenge of an ageing population first needs to be recognised, and then met. The figures point to a potential catastrophe in how the State will be able to cope. This year, over 10,000 people will celebrate their 100th birthday. By 2036, that figure is due to rise to 100,000 and will reach 500,000 by 2066. Over the longer term, it has been estimated that more than 11 million people alive today – 17 per cent of the population – can expect to live to more than 100 years old. The figures published by the Department for Work and Pensions predict that a baby boy born in 2011 will live for an average of just under ninety years, compared with just over ninety-two years and six months for a baby girl.

An extra 1.4 million people will turn sixty-five between 2011 and 2016. Yet proposals set out in the Dilnot report will only cover critical and high-level care. It does not take into account residential care, or how families can prevent the family home being sold to pay for it.

Few immediate solutions present themselves, apart from the obvious concern that people need to take responsibility and recognise that they need to prepare for old age by saving now. Government could assist with this by creating senior citizen bonds, with tax incentives to save and pay into a scheme which would mature upon retirement. By these means, a savings culture for old age might be created, helping to alleviate the crisis we face.

There should also be a responsibility on the part of adults to take a greater role in the care of their parents. We have got an absurd situation in which it is assumed to always be the State's responsibility to look after the old, rather than that of their children. In comparison to

Asian countries such as Japan, which have a tradition of caring for their elderly as an automatic duty, our preoccupation on the nuclear family has excluded the elderly from modern society and the family unit. Historically, families had a duty to take care of their elderly members, yet we seem to have rejected the idea that as individuals we may have obligations that may not be of our own volition, and instead transferred these obligations to government.

This must change. It is the role of government to help to foster these responsibilities, especially when it comes to caring for our elderly.

We can do this through the tax system, particularly council tax. For example, with tax credits for every family who cares for an elderly relative at home. This should be cost-effective for local authorities who will be under greater pressure to provide for care placements.

While it would not tackle the issue of elderly people who need high-level care in the case, for example, of dementia, it would begin to restore that sense of duty towards the elderly who have looked after us.

SUMMARY AGENDA
- We need to end the 'hand out' culture. We should introduce greater conditionality and time limits into the welfare system.
- We should establish a new 'Right to Own' principle within our social housing sector.
- We need to create a welfare system more in accordance with the fluid nature of modern employment. The government should create a new Baby Bonus, instead of maternity pay. We should create new tax incentives for those who look after the elderly in their own home.

6. Health: The NHS in a Changing World

Delivering an NHS for the twenty-first century

The NHS is more than the sum of its parts. Not only has it become a treasured national institution, it has become one of the most crucial 'points of contact' between the State and the individual. The NHS also embodies the hope of successive generations. It gives comfort and support for a mother giving birth, and for a dying old man in the last weeks of life. Over a million people work in the NHS because they choose to: they have a vocation to care, to save and improve the lives of patients daily. Polling data demonstrates that it ranks as a top priority for voters across the political spectrum, yet despite a renewed commitment to protecting the NHS, the Conservative Party consistently lags behind the Labour Party with regard to public confidence on the issue.[78]

The NHS Constitution lays out seven core principles:

The NHS provides a comprehensive service, available to all.

---

78 http://lordashcroft.com/pdf/14052011_general_population_10k_poll_tables.pdf, pg 461

Access to NHS services is based on clinical need, not an individual's ability to pay.

The NHS aspires to the highest standards of excellence and professionalism.

NHS services must reflect the needs and preferences of patients, their families and their carers.

The NHS works across organisational boundaries and in partnership with other organisations in the interest of patients, local communities and the wider population.

The NHS is committed to providing best value for taxpayers' money and the most effective, fair and sustainable use of finite resources.

The NHS is accountable to the public, communities, and patients that it serves.[79]

We firmly believe that the Conservative Party must remain committed to an NHS that follows these principles, which nearly everybody accepts. Equally, it is also important that we continue to reform, and ensure that the NHS of the twenty-first century is ready to face the tough challenges ahead.

It is clear that reform of our public services cannot be delivered without the support of the professionals working with them. Reform will only be successful where NHS professionals and workers are given a voice, and, above all, a sense that reform is not something to be feared, but welcomed. In finding new ways of discovering how to deliver most efficient pathways of care and treatment, NHS professionals hold the key to unlocking the best possible practices.

At the same time reform is not something that can be achieved with one big bang; it is a principle which must be constantly applied. If we are to move forward in

---

79   The NHS Constitution, 2010

delivering the best possible public services, we must never let our foot off the pedal. Each generation of politicians must look again at what works and what now needs to change. We must constantly learn from past experience to drive new innovations and new methods, to continually ask ourselves how we can make things better, to ensure that we achieve value for money. Reform is driven by momentum, not speed: if we are to win the trust of professionals and the public, we must do so by setting out a clear and consistent case.

The starting point for how we can deliver a better NHS must begin with a simple question: how can we provide better healthcare for all, that will not only improve and extend quality of life, but will ensure greater equity and that the needs of all the population are met?

The NHS and our public services face a common problem. We are paying more for these services, yet this extra money is actually purchasing less. And while performance management has improved across public service providers, this has focused on removing the worst rather than allowing the best to grow. There has been a failure to establish any connection between this performance management and the allocation of resources. This requires a focus on unit costs, essential for any improvement in productivity. Yet little attention is paid to this. Instead, obligations to deliver are entirely divorced from budgets, the former being set by inspectorates and departments, the latter being a historic budget set by the Treasury, usually with a bit extra for inflation. Data might be collected, but it has little to no impact on whether spending is really achieving value for money.

Instead there have been large increases in funding, with the result that many providers simply receive more money for doing the same thing. This increases inefficiency and diminishes productivity. The urgent situation is unsustainable: while UK private sector productivity increased by 20 per cent between 1997 and 2007, public sector productivity fell by 3.4 per cent, with NHS productivity declining by 4.3 per cent.[80] It has been estimated that this has resulted in the State spending £60 billion more than it needs to each year. The productivity challenge we face is perhaps most stark in the NHS. If the average NHS hospital was as efficient as those in top quartile, then the NHS could provide 27 per cent more treatments.[81]

The situation may get worse. In the last twenty years of life, nearly everyone suffers from at least one condition that requires regular medical intervention. By 2030, the number of people over 85 in the UK is expected to double. New technology like MRI scanners continues to increase the cost of health further, making up half the annual increases in spending. Furthermore, each year the price of new drugs adds several hundred million to the NHS's burdens. Altogether, under current projections, the NHS is projected to require in real terms £230 billion in 2030, or twice its current budget.[82]

Over the past thirteen years, under the previous Labour government, healthcare spending rose sharply from £38 billion in 1997 to £102 billion. Some of this increase was necessary and welcome. Despite this,

---

80 Phelps M., 'Total public service output and productivity', UK Centre for the Measurement of government Activity, Office for National Statistics, 2009

81 KPMG, 'Payment for Success- How to shift power from Whitehall to public service customers', pg 5

82 Lansley, Andrew, 'Why the health service needs surgery', *Daily Telegraph*, 1 June 2011

in comparison to other developed nations, the NHS remains chronically underfunded. As a proportion of GDP, we spent 8.7 per cent in 2008. This is the same as Ireland, yet far behind other countries such as France, Germany and The Netherlands, who have kept spending on healthcare far higher over decades.

Costs on crucial treatments have also not kept pace with overall spending on the NHS. While annual public spending per capita has risen from $1,195 to $2,585, the percentage spent on pharmaceutical treatments has fallen from 15.9 per cent to 11.8 per cent. In France, by comparison, a rise of $1,775 to $2,875 has seen the proportion of pharmaceutical spending rise from 15 per cent to 16.4 per cent.

Perhaps more crucially, we have seen critical outcomes in healthcare deteriorate compared to other developed countries. A recent Lancet study of the UK, Australia, Canada, Denmark, Norway and Sweden showed us lagging well behind on five year cancer survival rates, over a twelve-year period from 1995–2007. Indeed, the study goes on to suggest that had NHS perform-ance matched that of the highest performing countries analysed, around 11,400 deaths from cancer would have been avoided.[83] While mortality rates from cancer are falling, the UK remains well above the European average and the gap is not closing.[84] The UK only has 5.6 MRI units per million people, with the OECD average being 12.5, and 7.4 CT scanners per million people, a figure again dwarfed by the OECD average of 23.8.[85] The NHS

---

83   http://www.lshtm.ac.uk/eph/ncde/cancersurvival/icbp_paper1.pdf
84   Featherstone, et al., 2010
85   OECD Health Data 2010, 'How does the UK Compare?', http://www.oecd.org/dataoecd/46/4/38980557.pdf

still suffers from wide variations in care: the average length of a stay for a broken hip ranges from 10.9 days in the best hospitals to 44.5 in the worst. One estimate suggests that 40 per cent of patients are in hospital beds unnecessarily.[86] Moreover, despite the amount of the increase in spending devoted to increasing the number of staff, the UK still remains significantly below the rest of the OECD when it comes to practicing physicians – 2.6 per 1,000 people, compared to an average of 3.2 per thousand across the 34 OECD countries.[87]

As the OECD has said, 'the quantity and quality of [British] health care services remain lower than the OECD average.'[88] It suffers from the problems of any large monopoly, state or private. It is inefficient, slow to innovate, and suffers from poor customer service.

It is clear that a lack of efficiency in spending is not only detrimental to the public purse, but to patients themselves. Using 'mortality amenable to healthcare' as a basis for comparison, described as the number of deaths that can reasonably be expected to be avoided as a result of care, we are falling behind our European counterparts. One study demonstrated that in 2004, there were 17,157 deaths that could have been avoided, had the rate of amenable mortality matched the average of France, Germany, Spain and The Netherlands.[89] In terms of percentages, after seven years of additional spending on

---

86 Reform, 2011, pg 5

87 OECD Health Data 2010, 'How does the UK Compare?', http://www.oecd.org/dataoecd/46/4/38980557.pdf

88 Reform, 2011, pg 3

89 Matthew Sinclair 'Wasting Lives, a statistical analysis of NHS performance in a European context since 1981' Taypayers' Alliance, 2008 pg 4

the NHS, amenable mortality was 26.9 per cent higher than the average across the five European countries.[90]

Recent British performance in healthcare has been disappointing. There remain great efficiency gains to be made within the NHS, particularly in areas such as procurement and tariff reform. Yet productivity and efficiency savings will only get us so far. It is undeniable that at some stage, all parties will need to face the greatest challenge that is confronting the NHS: that with an ageing population and rising levels of chronic illness brought on by diseases of lifestyle choice, the NHS will reach a point that it is unable to provide the healthcare that the public expects. How can we ensure that the NHS continues to survive for the next fifty years without simply going bust? It is to other countries that we must look to find the answers.

A Care Revolution

Talk to any medical professional, specialist or staff in the NHS and they will tell you the same thing. The NHS, or rather its public perception, is geared around hospital and acute provision, when what we need to recognise is that, in the twenty-first century, hospitals are no longer places where many of their current patients should be. Of course, no one would deny that there are genuine reasons why many patients should be there: some have been rushed into the emergency room, while others with life-threatening conditions are waiting for an operation. For people in these situations, every hospital bed is desperately needed. In the previous century, a measure

---

90   Matthew Sinclair 'Wasting Lives, a statistical analysis of NHS performance in a European context since 1981' Taypayers' Alliance, 2008 pg 10

of political success would have been how many beds a hospital might have. We can no longer continue to play this game. Every single piece of medical evidence points to one simple fact: the greater the number of patients lying on a hospital bed or a hospital trolley in a corridor at any one time, the greater the failure of our healthcare system to deliver effective and preventative care that saves lives.

Kaiser Permanente is a non-profit health maintenance organisation originally established in California in 1945 to offer pre-paid medical care to construction and shipyard workers. It now has over 8 million members, owns and manages hospitals, combining health insurance with an exclusive relationship with large physician group practices known as Permanente Medial Groups. As an integrated financing and healthcare delivery group, it is perhaps more similar to the NHS than other US healthcare organisations.

Yet Kaiser Permanente has a motto: 'Unplanned hospital admissions are a sign of system failure.' Patients who did require such unplanned treatment, Kaiser believe, did not receive the best care at an earlier stage. Instead, the organisation's focus is on care on the ground, above all integration of care: allowing patients to move between hospitals, where there was active management of patients; placing common conditions such as hip replacements on care pathways; making use of general physicians known as 'hospitalists' to work in the inpatient environment. Above all underpinning Kaiser's model of care was the idea of 'multispeciality' – medical practices where specialists work alongside generalists. Doctors, rather than managers, take on leadership roles within these medical groups, and in doing so are actively committed to their success. Unlike the NHS, there is little sense of a false wall between primary and secondary care since Kaiser's care integration pathways straddle that divide.

The results? Kaiser patients use three and a half times fewer bed days than NHS patients. In other words, system failure in the NHS is three and a half times worse. The figures quite simply speak for themselves. In 2007/08 there were 4.75 million unplanned hospital admissions in the NHS. This represents 65 per cent of all hospital bed days in England.

If we are to have a responsible and informed debate on the future of the NHS, we must accept that the future of the nation's health begins with the promotion not only of preventative health, but in particular the management of long-term conditions in the best possible setting for patients. It is our duty to ensure that, as technology develops, the focus of the NHS becomes one of patient care. Foremost, delivery of quality care should be the most important consideration for our understanding of healthcare. In essence, care in itself is not something which is to be given to patients in addition to medication or treatment; care in itself must be recognised for the value it provides, not just for the patient themselves, but also for the value it brings in lowering costs, ensuring that the NHS can continue to survive into the twenty-first century.

Camden is one of the poorest cities in the United States, with nearly 95 per cent of the population eligible for Medicaid assistance. Its hospitals were under ever greater pressure from rising demand: admissions to emergency departments increased by 20 per cent between 1992 and 2001. Overcrowding at Camden's Emergency Departments was becoming a significant problem. One hospital was designed to accommodate 22,000 visits per year, yet was handling 56,000 in 2008, up from 51,000 in 2007.

The situation became unsustainable, yet it took police reform to begin a healthcare revolution in Camden. Jeff Brenner, a family physician practicing in Camden, joined the board of a new police reform commission as one of its two citizen members. It opened his own eyes to new ideas, such as the work of former New York Police Commissioner William Bratton and his Compstat approach of mapping crime – and in doing so, focusing resources on hot spots. The reform commission suggested Camden Police Department to do the same, creating computerised crime maps, and in turn adapting police beats to focus on the 'worst' areas and the times at which crimes were most likely to occur there.

The police – or rather their unions – refused. So Brenner made his own maps. In particular, he wanted to find out the emergency room visits of victims of serious assault. He persuaded the three main local hospitals to give him access to their data, the medical billing records which Brenner was able to transfer onto a desktop and begin to analyse the data. The deeper he delved into the data, Brenner quickly moved beyond assault patterns. A far more interesting pattern began to emerge from the lines on the spread sheets: the pattern of how patients flowed in and out of Camden's hospitals.

Take injuries relating to falls, for example. Mapping the data available in the same way crime maps operate showed instantly that a single high-rise building in Camden was responsible for more of its residents being rushed to hospital with serious falls – fifty-seven elderly people in two years – than any other in the city. The falls in that building were responsible so far for nearly $3 million in health bills.

It wasn't long before Brenner was adopting the Compstat approach to police reform to Camden's own healthcare, creating his own Healthstat maps. Each block, was analysed using data gathered from medical claims data from three nearby hospitals and emergency departments over a five year period from 2002 to 2007. In total, 387,000 records for 98,000 patients were analysed.

The results were startling. 80 per cent of the total healthcare costs were generated by just 13 per cent of the 98,000 patients. In all, 20 per cent of the population was responsible for 90 per cent of all healthcare costs. And yet the problem was far worse than this. Taking the top 1 per cent of patients who were most frequently admitted to hospital, the team were able to reveal that this tiny group of 1,035 patients made 39,056 hospital visits over five years. They accounted for 10 per cent of all admissions. They generated charges of a total of $375 million – 30 per cent of Camden's total medical costs. Using the available data, it was possible to turn a microscope on this small group of what were labelled 'super users'. One patient alone was admitted to hospital or A&E 324 times over five years. Another was admitted to hospital no less than 113 times in a single year. Among the 1 per cent, the most expensive patient needed $3.5 million of medical care.

The two most expensive blocks in terms of healthcare provision were in north Camden. Brenner uncovered that 900 people living here accounted for 4,000 hospital visits (including the patient who had visited 324-times) between 2002 and 2008. They had cost over $2 million in healthcare bills.

Brenner wasn't interested in the cost. Indeed, cost – though crucial for ensuring the survival of our own

NHS – is of secondary concern. What matters is care. If we provide bad care, the effects can quickly be measured and defined by the number of patients admitted to A&E. Quality care, the type that is both timely and effective, prevents this, and in turn will reduce costs. Look after the patient, and the costs will look after themselves. We cannot escape the fact that those people with the worst care are often those whom we find rotating in and out of A&E's doors. As Brenner himself has remarked, 'Emergency room visits and hospital admissions should be considered failures of the heath-care system until proven otherwise.'

The Camden findings are by no means unique. In Austin, Texas, an analysis of patients by the Integrated Care Collaboration, a not for profit clinic providing care for uninsured patients, revealed that just nine patients were responsible for 2,678 visits to Austin-area Emergency Departments between 2003 and 2008, at a total cost of more than \$3 million. One patient alone made 145 emergency visits in the final year of the study. A separate study in California found that 1,000 'super users' each incurred costs of over \$100,000 in 2007. Nationally, further research has shown only 4 per cent of Medicaid patients had annual costs of more than \$25,000, and yet consumed 50 per cent of total Medicaid spending.

The mission for Brenner was clear. Find the patients with the highest medical costs; if he could do something to improve the quality of total care, perhaps he would be able to do something to prevent the massive dependency on emergency room use and reduce the overall costs to the Camden healthcare system. In 2007, Brenner launched the Citywide Care Management System (CCMS) to help solve the problem. A software programme was purchased to link the three hospital databases using name, address and date of birth. The data was updated every three to six months. Using just Microsoft Access, the team were able to analyse 480,000 individual claims for 90,000 patients between 2002 and 2009. The cost of creating the database was minimal but it took time, something which Brenner was impatient to waste. To begin with, he simply gathered together some social workers and A&E doctors, to whom he revealed the patterns he had found, explaining the cost statistics of the most expensive 1 per cent of super users. 'These are the people I want to help you with,' he pleaded. 'Introduce me to your worst-of-the-worst patients.'

They did. What Brenner found was perhaps predictable: patients with multiple chronic illnesses, problems with obesity, drugs, alcohol and unemployment. The referrals identified by doctors matched the cost statistics that Brenner had dug out.

The principle remains. The team actively seeks out clients, rather than what we might expect in most healthcare systems, including the NHS, where patients simply present themselves, often at A&E when their condition is already far advanced.

The Camden Coalition can't afford money for a clinic, so instead it relies upon phone calls and home visits. Every one of its 'super users' is given the team's urgent call number. Often this means that any health crisis can be dealt with immediately. Only rarely does it ever mean that the emergency room is required.

Above all, the programme only worked if effective relationships were formed between the patient and the team. 'The ones you build a relationship with,' Brenner says, 'you can change behaviour. Half we can build a relationship with. Half we can't.' In order to maximise the success of creating a bond between patient and the team, patient visits begin with two or three members of the team making contact, fostering that bond and ensuring that an immediate multidisciplinary approach is taken to the patient's condition. Whoever in the team creates the best bond with the patient then becomes the lead member for the patient's care.

In effect, the Camden Coalition was able to create its own healthcare service 'without walls'. By recruiting a team of the best primary care doctors, nurses and social workers within the neighbourhoods themselves, the programme was able to save millions. In effect, the Camden Coalition's ambition was to create an elite medical force.

The Camden Coalition was able to work with thirty-six super users in its original programme. Each month, these thirty-six patients alone were costing an average of $1.2million in hospital charges. After the intervention programme, charges per month fell by more than 56 per cent (a reduction of nearly $687,000 per month) while the number of monthly hospital visits fell by 40 per cent.

Was it worth it? The cost of the first year of the CCMS programme was $150,000, roughly $347 per patient per month. And yet the cost of each super-user in terms of A&E/hospital services fell from $33,333 per month to $14,250. For every dollar spent on the intensive case management programme, monthly hospital costs in Camden were reduced by $55.

The success the Camden Coalition has had with their programme of active intervention in case management has been replicated elsewhere. In San Francisco, focusing upon a group of patients who used A&E five times or more in the previous year led to a 40 per cent reduction in emergency visits, while median A&E costs were reduced by 47 per cent. In Scotland, a similar care management programme for patients who visited A&E ten times or more over a six month period reduced relevant emergency room visits from 720 to 499, a reduction of 31 per cent.

The benefits of such intervention programmes had an even greater effect in later years: two years on, in San Francisco, emergency room visits for those 'super-user' patients had decreased by 61 per cent, with cost reductions of 59 per cent. For inpatient admissions, these declined by 64 per cent with the number of impatient days down by 62 per cent – and inpatient costs down by 69 per cent. It seems that after a first year of intervention, their overall conditions had begun to stabilise, resulting in the dramatic reductions witnessed.

So why does the NHS fail to deliver care to those who need it most, and whose treatment would result in a significant change in outcomes for everybody, not just those with chronic conditions. Within the NHS, a commitment to a universal service free at the point of delivery has obscured the need to focus on patients who need immediate care, in the right place at the right time. Yet by treating the few, the healthcare of the many will improve at less cost to the system.

The NHS is divided between providing both primary and secondary care. To this we must add chronic care. We should look to creating health maps in the same way as the Camden coalition has done. We need to recognise that those patients with highly complex and chronic conditions represent a high-need, high-risk group whom we must seek out and treat urgently. This is not an argument about cost. It is a case for taking care seriously. And if we take care seriously, costs will inevitably be reduced as well.

Getting the data

The Camden Coalition would not have been possible without the available data which exposed the failure to deal effectively with 'super users'. How many similar areas of deprivation are there in the UK?

The truth is that we simply don't have the means of accessing data within the NHS to make such an analysis. We cannot therefore tackle the problems facing deprived communities in healthcare. Primary care data is available. In Northumberland for example, Medics Data has been used for over ten years as a tool for the development of chronic disease management. We just lack the vision and ability to scale up what works within the NHS, precisely because there is no incentive to roll out and expand best practice. This is beginning to change, with developments such as the Torbay Agreement, through which local trusts across Birmingham and Solihull agreed to share information, financial resources and clinical responsibility, 'wherever it is agreed this will improve the health and wellbeing of the people of Birmingham'.

The experience of the NHS IT system proves that statist, centralising approach to technological advancement was a costly failure. £13 billion has been spent, but in pilot sites only 4 per cent of patients seen in general practice out of hours have a record which is viewed by the clinician treating them. This figures drops to below 1 per cent in hospitals. We must allow innovation to take place from the ground up, with individual groups being given a goal but granted the freedom to reach it their own way. Though poor IT procurement has been a perennial source of waste in the NHS, an integrated system of healthcare will require effective use of technology, particularly in linking primary care providers with hospitals. In a world where people can carry out all of their banking and shopping online, the same could be true of healthcare. The NHS must embrace the internet, to allow patients to access their medical records remotely, order prescriptions, make appointments and communicate with their doctor – all through a secure online system.

Clearly central government would need to lay down basic guidelines, for example around working with different systems. However, IT contracts should not be being signed by Whitehall civil servants. Between 1994 and 2008, New Zealand managed to achieve a functioning system of electronic health records for 4.5 million citizens, at a cost of only £15 million, through precisely this approach.[91] Kaiser have also only been able to deliver their integrated healthcare approach through their HealthConnect programme which has involved investment in 'KP online'. This enables members to communicate by email, access medical records, make appointments and order prescription refills.

The pioneers of healthcare IT are in Denmark, where electronic health records have been in use for over a decade. Doctors send and receive all information about laboratory test results, referrals and prescriptions electronically, and receive automatic notification if one of their patients registers in a hospital's emergency department. This is how an efficient, joined-up system should work. It avoids reams of unnecessary paperwork. In Denmark, it is estimated that over 90 per cent of clinical communication between primary

---

91   Trisha Greenhalgh, Tom Bowden, 'Why many hands make IT work', *Health Service Journal*, 16 September 2010

care providers and secondary care providers takes place electronically. [92]

The same Commonwealth Fund study calculated that the Danish use of IT is so efficient that it saves doctors an average of 50 minutes per day[93], which would otherwise be taken up with administration. A 2008 report calculated that electronic record keeping saved Denmark's health system $120 million a year.[94]

In this new age where productivity and quality are highly prized, electronic record keeping should appeal to the NHS. This year Kable, the public sector consultancy, forecast that software investment in the NHS would rise from £86 million in 2007/08 to £365m in 2013/14 – an annual growth rate of 27 per cent.[95] The future of the NHS, and the cost savings it can make, lies in technology's hands. But there is an important lesson that Denmark teaches: electronic medical records only succeed as long as patients have control over their own records. This is the case at Kaiser Permanente, likewise at Beth Israel Deconess Hospital in Boston, one of the first US hospitals to adopt electronic health records a decade ago, where patients themselves choose to store their records using several different programmes, including Google Health or Microsoft Healthvault.

---

92   D. Protti and I. Johansen, Widespread Adoption of Information Technology in Primary Care Physician Offices in Denmark: A Case Study, The Commonwealth Fund, March 2010

93   D. Protti and I. Johansen, Widespread Adoption of Information Technology in Primary Care Physician Offices in Denmark: A Case Study, The Commonwealth Fund, March 2010

94   *New York Times*, 'Denmark Leads the Way in Digital Care', 12 January 2010

95   *Financial Times*, 'Healthcare systems open to a new generation', 16 June 2010

Facing the demographic challenge: funding the NHS for the future

The NHS needs to address issues of integrated care, focussing on chronic conditions and super users. It needs to effectively collect and analyse data in order for it to dispense treatment where it is most needed if it is to succeed in bringing down costs. Further reforms, such as extending payment by results, linking activity to budgets, are essential if we are to deliver service reform that will improve outcomes at the same time as decrease costs. Indeed, the entire direction of how we view what constitutes good public services needs to change. Instead of simply tackling underperforming trusts and hospitals, we need to start expanding good trusts and hospitals, rewarding them so that excellent practice is encouraged to spread and change the pattern of provision. While the 'floor' has been moved upwards, the ceiling has not.[96]

More sophisticated technology and better early diagnosis can deliver huge cost savings, but it is unlikely that these alone will be enough to ensure adequate investment in the NHS for the longer term. The demographic challenge, even in the next few years, is immense. Between 2011 and 2016 the number of people aged 65 and over will rise by 1.4 million. An ageing population will require ever greater healthcare provision. According to the OECD, healthcare spending will rise to 9.7 per cent of GDP by 2050, resulting in an annual increase in expenditure of £40 billion just to keep service provision at a constant level. At the same time, the diseases that we face are no longer ones of infection and chance, but increasingly they are diseases of lifestyle choice, in many cases entirely preventable. The Foresight Programme

---

96   See KPMG, Payment for Success, pg 7

projects that by 2050 there will be a 23 per cent increase in prevalence of obesity related strokes, a 34 per cent increase in obesity related hypertension, and a 98 per cent increase in obesity related diabetes.[97]

The scale of the fiscal challenge is immense. It is worth asking whether it is time for the relationship between individuals and their own contribution to their healthcare to be considered. As the IMF has warned, even successful reforms to healthcare delivery are unlikely to make healthcare sustainable. The IMF implies this might lead to 'a fundamental change in the role of the State in the provision of health services'.[98]

In the UK, we are unique in our dependence upon the State – i.e. the taxpayer – to foot the bill for the healthcare of even our wealthiest citizens. While many social insurance systems in Europe feature public finance of slightly more than 75 per cent, in the UK our health-care system relies upon the taxpayer for 82 per cent of its total healthcare bill. We must ask ourselves: if we are to meet the increased cost of nearly an additional 3 per cent GDP spending on health by 2050 merely through increased taxation, or if there is another way?

The unavoidable truth is that healthcare is always paid for by somebody. The NHS currently costs the taxpayer around £2,000 per person.

Neither does pumping more money into the system necessarily lead to better outcomes for people. The US spends twice as much as the UK on healthcare, and has very little difference in results. Across the world, there

---

97   'A high-performing NHS? A review of progress 1997–2010', The King's Fund 2010, pg 42

98   IMF 2010, Macro-Fiscal Implications of Health Care Reform in Advanced and Emerging Economies

is next to no correlation between the amount spent and the quality of healthcare provided. Other factors, such as environment and lifestyle, are far more important. One famous experiment by the RAND corporation in 1970s America randomly assigned different costs for healthcare over five years to 2,000 families. Those assigned low prices consumed on average 30 per cent more healthcare – but found no positive effect on their actual level of health.[99]

If government is paying for all healthcare, then at some point it becomes necessary to ration resources to make sure that health doesn't simply consume the entire economy.

There are two fundamental issues in any health system: how the system is organised, and how it is paid for. In order to reform the NHS for the long term, the government will need to ensure innovation on the supply side and that demand doesn't grow out of control.

The way we have run healthcare has stayed more or less the same for over sixty years. There is now a strong case for reform.

It is increasingly recognised that patients need to take more responsibility for their own health. The quality of your diet and exercise routine is far more important than the quality of your hospital. New technology, easier ways of processing data and innovative websites like PatientsLikeMe, allow patients to control and monitor their own condition. In the long term, improvements in personal DNA sequencing could lead to an era of far more personalised medicine.

Some of these changes may prove to be passing fads rather than fundamental modifications in the way health

---

99   http://www.cato-unbound.org/2007/09/10/robin-hanson/cut-medicine-in-half/

works. If, however, we expect the NHS to take advantage of any of them, we will require a far more innovative and dynamic health sector than we have now. To create such a sector will, in turn, require the possibility of more competition and experimentation.

Innovation in new healthcare drugs and techniques can be conceived as consisting of two stages. First, there is the fundamental basic scientific research that is often led by universities and, due to its non-commercial nature, requires government support. But beyond this there is also a second stage in implementation, where new ideas are diffused and adopted throughout the rest of the system. It is this second stage that centralised systems such as the NHS are particularly bad at. In 2008, for example, the NHS spent £2.4 billion on the creation of new ideas, but just £0.15 billion on their spread and implementation.[100]

The NHS is unique in that the government runs the system completely and is frequently the single payer for all procedures as well. The result is that the NHS is a colossal organisation, famously the largest single employer in Western Europe. The NHS now employs 1.6 million people. Their wage costs make up 40 per cent of the NHS budget and the simple, automatic increases in their wages cost £420 million a year.[101] There is a suspicion that sometimes the system meets the needs of its staff more than its customers. English GPs are the best paid in the world, taking in average pay of £105,148 in 2006, around twice as much as the £55,696 average in Germany or £45,696 in France.[102]

---

100   Barlow, et al., 2008, pg 8
101   Featherstone, et al., 2010, pg 1
102   Reform, 2011, pg 8

Before undertaking reform, it is always worth considering the benefits of what we have now. The chief merit of the NHS is that it is relatively cheap. By international standards, the NHS has a low budget but achieves average results. While the NHS can be strictly authoritarian in reducing choice and limiting options, this helps keep budgets down. A crucial task for any healthcare reform must be to make sure that we don't endanger this, and introduce a cycle of ever increasing costs.

The easiest reforms to implement would be on the supply side of the NHS and would be an extension of recent governments' work. The current monolith should be broken up. Hospitals should be given their independence, extending the Foundation Hospital model – initially controversial but now almost universally accepted. New non-profit and private operators should be allowed into the service, and, indeed, should compete on price. The actual commissioning and control of budgets should be delegated down to the lowest level possible – most likely to the patient themselves and the professional they trust most, their doctor. In surveys, 94 per cent of patients say that they have trust and confidence in their GP.[103] Patients should be given more choice over their GP and hospital. At the moment, only 8 per cent of patients a year are ever offered any sort of choice in the NHS.[104]

Such reforms have already been shown to work. For example, in Manchester, one Practice-Based Commissioning Group has reduced hospital admissions by 53 per cent, saving £300,000 a year.[105] Across the world, countries with more competition, such as

---

103   Norridge, 2011, pg 11
104   Featherstone, et al., 2009, pg 6
105   Norridge, 2011, pg 5

Germany and Switzerland, tend to be more efficient.[106] Two thirds of German hospitals are run privately or not-for-profit.[107] Patient satisfaction is the same in private and public hospitals.[108]

The practical difficulties of such reforms have been overstated. Some have argued that the private sector could only make profits by 'creaming off' the easiest patients, but experience so far shows this not to be the case. In 2009–2010, the largest group of patients in private care were those with learning difficulties and mental illness.[109]

The implementation of these reforms would simply be updating the NHS to the standard European model. This vision is more or less shared by reformist politicians in all three parties. While they are sure to be initially opposed by unions and opportunistic politicians, in the long term if pursued sensitively and on an evolutionary basis, they are likely to be achieved.

Far more difficult is the next stage of the reforms, which will need to look at how we fund healthcare.

Partly because the NHS has to compete with other areas of public spending, resources for healthcare have been tied to the traditional cycle of boom and bust funding. This is entirely dependent upon the policies of whichever party is in office and the current state of the national economy. The result of this has been the creation of an organisation that is subjected to countless reorganisations. These simply create a plethora of quangos and unaccountable middle-level managerial bodies. At the same time, we have fewer doctors and nurses per head

---

106   Reform, 2011, pg 3
107   Reform, 2011, pg 5
108   Reform, 2011, pg 2
109   Reform, 2011, pg 3

of the population than other developed countries. We have a massive shortage in diagnostic testing equipment, and a chronic underinvestment in our healthcare service which spends around 8 per cent of GDP compared to an average of nearer 12 per cent in other countries. The reality is that, with an ageing population and a rise in chronic diseases such as obesity, alcohol related illness and diabetes, the NHS is going to need much more cash if it is to survive for the next twenty years. The question that all politicians must ask themselves over the next ten years is: if we all agree, how can we get more money into the NHS without relying on the fickle mood of the Treasury to deliver only modest increases in spending?

We believe in the core principles of the NHS set out in the NHS constitution. This commitment must be the starting point for any serious approach to healthcare reform. If we are to deliver increased resources to match increased demands, we must always stick to the absolute principle that each and every person should be able to access high quality health services, regardless of the ability to pay. Indeed, the success of any new healthcare system must be judged on how it provides for those on the lowest incomes in society.

Talking quality of life and death
When is it ever acceptable to talk about death?

End of life care is a topic that very few people want talk about. Equally, death isn't a subject which we expect the NHS to deal with: our healthcare service is geared to prolonging life, fighting to keep a dying patient alive for as long as possible. No one wishes to tell a patient or their family that there is nothing more that can be done. So the fight goes on. Increased doses of drugs with unknown effectiveness are administered; tumours are once again operated on, intravenous feeding tubes are inserted as the body of a terminally ill patient slowly gives up that fight.

And while we focus on getting the best possible medicines and treatment for terminally ill patients, it's perhaps easy to overlook that the NHS should be about ensuring that patients have as good quality of death as they do a quality of life. Yet end of life care doesn't often feature in discussions about the future of the NHS. This is despite the fact that end of life care costs billions of pounds per year. Cancer patients alone, who constitute 27 per cent of deaths, are estimated to cost a total of £1.8 billion for their final twelve months.[110] Equally, NHS spending is only a portion of the total cost of end of life care. At present, independent hospices provide 2,150 inpatient beds, whereas NHS hospices provide 450. This ratio is borne out by the funding arrangements for individual hospices, which on average receive 26 per cent of their income from PCTs – £130 million out of a total of £500 million, with the rest coming from other sources.[111]

In 2008, only 4 per cent of people died in a hospice,[112] 95 per cent of these were cancer patients.[113] In fact, patients with other terminal illnesses are significantly underrepresented among those who receive specialist palliative care: less than 1 per cent of patients in a hospice had circulatory and respiratory diseases. The stark and uncomfortable truth is that each year, thousands of patients whose remaining life should be spent in the most

---

110   National Audit Office, *End of Life Care,* 2008, pg 5

111   National Audit Office, *End of Life Care,* 2008, pg 7

112   National Audit Office, *End of Life Care,* 2008, pg 5

113   Royal College of Physicians, *Palliative Care Services, Meeting the Needs of Patients,* 2007, pg 3

comfortable surroundings possible are instead dying on trolleys in hospitals utterly unsuited to providing the best possible care. Equally disturbing is the cost of providing this unsuitable care: one report put the estimated cost of providing care to cancer patients in the last year of life at £14,236 per patient, a total of around £1.8 billion for the 127,000 patients.[114] For the wrong care, this is a huge price to pay.

If we believe in an NHS that is not just about making people better, but about looking after every single patient, improving quality of care in the NHS, particularly for patients with a terminal illness, is an essential concern. Quality of death must be considered as important as quality of life.

The fact that so few terminally ill patients enrol in hospices until the very last stages of life is not a phenomenon confined to the NHS. In the US, the insurance company Aetna noticed that just 26 per cent of their policyholders with a life expectancy of less than a year had enrolled in a hospice. Instead, nearly three-quarters were continuing with intensive curative care programmes that inevitably were having little effect. Aetna realised that few patients would be willing to give up the opportunity of a cure to enter a hospice, so in 2004 they decided to allow a group of policy holders to receive hospice services without giving up other treatments. A two year study of the results found that patients were far more likely to have entered a hospice; enrolments were up at 70 per cent. The patients' use of hospitals fell by more than two thirds, while A&E visits fell by 50 per cent. Overall costs for patients fell by 25 per cent.

---

114   http://www.nao.org.uk/idoc.ashx?docId=3bec862c-1aed-4019-965f-3a76910ca834&version=-1

The results were so overwhelming that Aetna extended the trial. This time patients had to make a choice between curative care programmes and entering a hospice. Whatever the decision, patients were to receive regular phone calls from palliative care nurses to help them find whatever services they needed. The results were the same. The use of hospital services dropped, particularly among the elderly whose use of intensive care units fell by more than 85 per cent. Hospice enrolment rose by 70 per cent, and with it satisfaction levels of the patients themselves.

What was the secret of the programme's success? Just talking, it seems. By giving patients the simple opportunity to speak with an experienced and knowledgeable person about their needs on a daily basis, it was possible for the patients themselves to express what they wanted.

And yet when are those conversations ever had? In the US, two-thirds of terminally ill cancer patients in the Coping with Cancer Study reported that they had had no discussion with their doctor about their end of life care, despite being on average just four months from death. In Britain, the situation is little better – the very fact that only around 20 per cent of cancer patients die at home, compared to 45 per cent in the Netherlands and 58 per cent in Italy suggests a lack of appropriate information, since the majority of people when asked express a wish to die at home.[115] Perhaps a cultural reticence to discuss death is to blame, as much as the shortcomings of palliative care.

Yet talking about one's quality of death matters.

The elderly residents of La Crosse care home, Wisconsin, might seem to any medical analyst a statistical

---

115   Royal College of Physicians, *Palliative Care Services, Meeting the Needs of Patients*, 2007, pg 10

freak. According to Atul Gawande's article, 'Hospice medical care for dying patients', they spend half as many days in hospital compared to the average. And despite average rates of obesity and other lifestyle choices such as smoking, their life expectancy is over a year higher than the national average, and they have dramatically lower end-of-life hospital costs. At the nearby local hospital, none of its patients in Intensive Care beds are battling terminal illness, or suffering from the final stages of age related illness such as chronic heart failure or dementia. Those who are there have a chance of recovery. In contrast, in the UK, one study of a Primary Care Trust in October 2007 found that 40 per cent of patients who died in hospital did not have medical needs requiring hospital treatment, and that one in four of these patients had been there over a month.[116]

So what makes La Crosse so different? According to Gawande's research, it all goes back to 1991 when the local medical authorities launched a campaign to get doctors and their patients to discuss their end of life choices: in other words, what quality of death they would like. Within four years, it had become routine for patients admitted to a hospital or a home to be asked four questions:

Do you want to be resuscitated if your heart stops?

Do you want treatments such as intubation and mechanical ventilation?

Do you want antibiotics?

Do you want tube or intravenous feeding if you can't eat on your own?

According to the critical-care specialist who works at the nearby hospital to La Crosse, Dr Gregory Thompson,

---

116   National Audit Office, *End of Life Care*, 2008, pg 7

the answers to these questions 'are not laid out in stone. But instead of having the discussion when they get to the intensive care unit, we find many times it has already taken place.' And of course the answers to the questions change as people's own minds change. But what matters most is having the discussion in the first place. At La Crosse people are far more likely to have given thought to what they do and don't want before the crisis of death appears. As a result, La Crosse has record patient satisfaction and its costs for end of life care are down to under half the national average. Yet as Gawande admits in his article, 'It was that simple, and that complicated.' There is no way around the extremely difficult and upsetting fact that many patients come to hospital and the NHS to die. But that should not prevent us from having that conversation about how quality of death really does matter.

SUMMARY AGENDA
- We should continue the current successful reform programme in the NHS, allowing successful hospitals to expand and weaker hospitals to close. We should take advantage of the extra efficiencies private sector companies can provide.
- We should seek to improve the quality of end of life care. In particular, we should make sure all patients are given the chance to discuss their own individual preferences for their quality of death as early as possible.

7. Education: Increasing Educational Standards

An Australian teacher who recently came to England notices her new students are less motivated than their Australian counterparts; also, they don't remember what they have been taught. She spends her weekends preparing lessons, whereas in Australia they would use an established text book. Her department head urges her to 'experiment' rather than using the tried and tested methods.

A twenty-one year old who has just graduated is the first of her generation to go to university. The subject was Media Studies. She thought this would lead to a job in journalism. It hasn't.

A primary school class of eight year olds is being taught multiplication. They input the numbers into a calculator – out pops the result – it's magic. That's the way they will do maths in the future.

These are snapshots of an education system that has lost its way. Responsibility for motivating pupils has been taken away from teachers and has been put on making subjects 'relevant' or paying students to go to school. Examiners are prevented from using subjective judgement and are unable to single out a good essay because it doesn't tick the right boxes.

These deficiencies in the British educational system have been compounded by the nature of the academic experience typical of English universities. The Higher Education Policy Institute has conducted surveys since 2006 in order to find how satisfied they are with their academic experience. The report concluded that there are significant differences between Britain and other European countries when it comes to contact hours and private study; British university students spent an average of 29 hours per week studying, which compares badly to their Swiss or French counterparts who on average study for 38 and 39 hours per week respectively.

The rise of the US in the twentieth century shows how important education can be; comparatively more US students were graduating from high school and college than other nations and so were able to outperform Europe and Asia economically. Towards of the end of the century however, the performance of the US stagnated and it was overtaken by Asian countries with a strong focus on education. European competitors also caught up, but unfortunately Britain was not one of these competitors as we focused on increasing quantity rather than improving quality in education.

When the international OECD league table PISA (Programme for International Student Assessment) survey came out in 2000 Germany's poor performance was the subject of national outcry and sparked significant reform and improvement. In 2010 Britain lies at twenty-eighth in mathematics, twenty-fifth in reading and sixteenth in science in the same table, and yet there is complacency about our system.

Creating more good schools

The divide between our government and independently run schools is growing. Our independent schools continue to be among the best internationally. Across the world, parents seek to send their children to them. It cannot be right that the only way to secure a good education in areas of Britain is to pay for it.

Britain has become a less meritocratic country since the rise of the flawed egalitarian consensus of the 1960s. Although unpopular, grammar schools gave working class children a historically unequalled chance to get the best in academic education. By the end of the 1960s, only 38 per cent of places at Oxford were afforded to privately educated pupils. The proportion is now back up to around 50 per cent.[117]

British politics has never been particularly logical about education, and in no area is this truer than the issue of grammar schools. While selection by ability for secondary schools remains taboo, selection by ability for universities is seen as no more than best practice. At the very least, we should look into expanding currently successful grammar schools.

Indeed, while selection by ability may have disappeared from many regions of the country, selection by income continues to increase. Desperate middle class parents move to expensive new houses to ensure that they are in the catchment area of the local good school. Other parents coincidentally seem to rediscover their faith shortly before their child applies to attend a religious school.

---

117   http://www.spectator.co.uk/coffeehouse/6843638/does-davis-have-a-point-about-grammar-schools.thtml

A good education should not be tied to religious enthusiasm, houses or exams. There is no actual limit on good schools. Our economy does not seem to have discovered any analogous limit of good supermarkets or good cinemas. Every parent who wants to send their child to a strong, academic school should be able to do so.

While we should be proud to provide every child with an education, we should not pretend that the public takeover of education has been without its problems. Without the discipline of consumer choice, bad schools have survived for far too long. Innovation has been slow or non-existent. Schools have served government targets rather than the interests of their parents and pupils.

The current Free Schools and Academies programmes of the coalition are excellent reforms. By breaking up the government's monopoly over education, they allow schools more independence and the freedom to implement new ideas. Already, the latest statistical evidence shows that academies are making a difference – improving the performance both of their own pupils and those in schools around them.[118] The nine schools of the Harris Federation have seen a 10 per cent improvement in the number of pupils obtaining five good GCSEs. The ARK academies have seen a 13 per cent increase.[119] Mossbourne Academy replaced Hackney Downs, once considered the worst school in Britain; 41 per cent of

---

118 Machin, Stephen and Vernoit, James, Changing School Autonomy: Academy Schools and their Introduction to England's Education, 2011

119 http://www.spectator.co.uk/coffeehouse/6226873/todays-gcse-results-prove-that-academies-work.thtml

its pupils are on free school meals and yet this year ten of them have been offered a place at Cambridge. The year before, only 40 children out of the 80,000 on free school meals across the country were offered places to Oxford or Cambridge.[120]

Nonetheless, such reforms will only ever have a limited effect unless we allow new schools to make a profit. It is understandable that the government is afraid of the political implications of profit making schools. Nevertheless, unless such schools are allowed to make a surplus, to form chains and spread best practices, we will never be able to replicate innovation on the scale needed to tackle the current problems in our schools.

At the moment many companies are involved in making money from state education; books, exams, management services and educational structures. It is intellectually dishonest to not allow profit making schools but allow this other activity. We should allow schools to specialise and select with a view to maximising educational potential.

A similar political dynamic exists in our university sector. The government's current reforms aim to create more independence for the sector, and give students more responsibility for their own education. Universities are able to charge higher fees, but students only ever have to pay the loan back if and when they are earning sufficient wages. Unfortunately, there is a real worry that the many limitations that the government have been forced to adapt in this policy will slow down the needed reforms. Our universities will not be able to obtain the

---

120 http://blogs.telegraph.co.uk/news/katharinebirbals-
ingh/100073221/the-state-sector-can-improve-its-schools-
when-its-leaders-throw-away-the-liberal-agenda/

funding they need, nor will competition drive efficiency, until universities are fully able to set their own fees.

We should be under no doubt that academics, activists and even many students unions were not so much opposed to the reforms due to increase in fees, as they were the idea of 'marketisation' itself. The coalition government's reforms are similar to the Graduate Tax that many on the left claim to approve of. The only difference is that rather than putting a central government bureaucracy in charge, the reforms gave power to the students and the universities. The income-conditional nature of the loans meant that costs should never put anyone off attending a university. The only reason for the less well-off to be discouraged was the irresponsible rhetoric of the academic establishment.

Improving teaching

In order to improve our education more generally, it is not just schools and parents that need to take more individual responsibility but children themselves. The academic experience needs to be far more individually tailored to the needs of each pupil. Partly that means better use of streaming within schools, but there are often also underexploited opportunities from new technology as well.

We should change our excuses culture and put responsibility on students to take forward their own education. People should not be bribed to attend school or university but feel it is a privilege. They should take responsibility for choosing courses rather than being 'advised and guided'. Our current system takes the focus away from individual endeavour. There is a strong case for schools allowing students to progress through school only when they 'pass' the year to create an incentive for harder work.

In many ways, too much of our education system is stuck in the medieval model where a single lecturer dictates to a single room of pupils. Personal guidance is given rarely and long after any particular piece of work is attempted. Only individual tutors or Oxbridge colleges have the man hours to really pursue one to one learning.

We can do better than this. Already on the internet, sites like Academic Earth are allowing anyone with a web browser to watch lectures from the leading academics of Harvard, Yale or Oxbridge. Other sites such as Khan Academy treat more basic subjects such as algebra or the French Revolution. They provide interactive tests allowing pupils to master each topic in their own time. Comprehensive data on where each pupil is excelling and where they are struggling is continually given to their tutor.

We will never fully replace teachers. No computer can yet mark an essay or answer every question a pupil might have. But technology now makes it far easier for teachers to focus their efforts on where they make the most difference, helping pupils when they get into real difficulties. The lessons from other industries suggest that the best way to improve efficiency is to systematise what is standard, and allow trained individuals to use their initiative where a more personal touch is required.

One problem we currently face is that too often the practice of teaching has become political. It has become a matter of ideology on what methods to use in teaching children how to read, or what elements of British history should be studied.

This is unfortunate. Politicians are not expected to be experts on the best means of performing heart operations, and they should not have to be experts on the relative merits of synthetic and analogue phonetics either. The best methods to teach children should be tested by exactly the same methods we use to test new medical treatments: through the scientific method, and randomly controlled trials.

Relying on ideology over evidence all too often just leads to a huge waste of public money. New Labour planned to spend over £50 billion on new school buildings, despite the statistical evidence that the effect of improved buildings on student attainment is very small.[121] Far more important to a school than the quality of the buildings is the quality of its teachers. Many of the schools in the Swedish Free School programme operated out of nothing more than an office block.

One reason ministers have felt the need to interfere, is that schools have seen themselves more as forces for social engineering than places to learn. The teachers unions have not helped, instinctively favouring an activist left wing view of society over the interests of their profession.

There continues to be a misguided belief in child centred education, when what children and their parents want is to be shown what knowledge and aptitudes are required. Why for example do British teachers spend huge amounts of time preparing lessons that are taught year after year when they could be learning from best practice?

School, of course, has to be about more than just earning grades, and schools do often have to be sensitive to those with troubled backgrounds. At the same

---

121 Quarmby, Katharine and Fazackerley, Anna,'Building Blocks? An Investigation Into Building Schools for the Future', Policy Exchange, 2009

time, schools simply cannot function without the ability to impose sufficient discipline. 80 per cent of teachers currently feel that their ability to teach is being harmed by pupils' bad behaviour.[122] A Freedom of Information request for the *Daily Mail* revealed that 1,145 weapons were confiscated off pupils between 2006 and 2010 – and this occurred despite the fact that until recently teachers were not allowed to look in pupils' bags.[123] Head teachers have to be given the power to impose discipline in their schools, and, if necessary, expel the worst offenders.

Examinations and Grades

Political forces in education even appear to have infected our public examination system. At present, there is a clear conflict of interest in the system, creating persistent grade inflation. Few have the incentive to really effectively complain about ever rising grades. It is far better for ministers, teachers, schools and parents to believe that the improvement is all real.

Of course some of the improvement may indeed be real. Nevertheless, Britain's continual slide down the world rankings suggests that the boost in grades do not seem to be crossing over into improvement in education more widely. Research by Professor Robert Coe of Durham University suggests that A-Levels are now two grades easier than they were twenty years ago.[124] When

---

122 Massey, Alex, 'Best Behaviour: School discipline, intervention and exclusion', Policy Exchange, 2011

123 http://www.dailymail.co.uk/news/article-2013781/Police-confiscated-1-000-deadly-weapons-children-school.html?ITO=1490

124 http://blogs.telegraph.co.uk/news/neilobrien1/100087875/q-are-exams-getting-easier-a-much-easier-at-the-top/

surveyed, 53 per cent of universities (and 100 per cent of the Russell Group) complained that grade inflation was making their job of choosing pupils harder.[125] The 2011 OECD Economy Survey of the UK complained that 'the share of A-Level entries awarded grade A has risen continuously for 18 years and has roughly trebled since 1980 ... independent surveys of cognitive skills do not support this development'.[126]

We need to remember that grades serve two different, if related, aims. The first is as a certification, to show that basic educational standards have been met. An analogous example is the driving test. Although we might be suspicious if an increase happened too fast, fundamentally it is a good thing if an ever increasing amount of people pass their driving test.

Crucially grades also serve a second function, acting as a measuring stick to compare our best performers and see how well as a nation we are doing compared to the past. We should be actively seeking to raise our own standards as countries in Asia are successfully doing. Meanwhile, our employers and universities need to be able to distinguish between our best performers.

We need to reform our grading system to help achieve this. One solution would be to return to the old system in which grades were given on a proportional basis, and, for example, the top 10 per cent of students are granted an A. Alternatively, we could keep the current system, but alongside a student's grades publish the percentage of other students who did better or worse. This would allow exams to serve both as a basic qualification and as

---

125 http://www.telegraph.co.uk/education/education-news/7872573/Universities-criticise-exam-grade-inflation.html
126 OECD Economic Surveys: United Kingdom, 2011, pg 89

and indication to employers of how well each student performed compared to their peer group.

Just as we helped tame monetary inflation through the creation of an independent central bank, we should look to tame grade inflation through the creation of an independent central examination board. This body should be free from the distortion of either government interference, or having to appeal to schools looking for lenient marking. While both schools and government would want some say in content and standards, the central focus of our independent body should be a board of the country's top universities, setting out exactly what level of knowledge they are looking for.

In countries leading in education there is a strong cultural assumption that a decent level of education is mandatory. The international evidence all suggests that a general education that can be flexible in the face of technical and social change proves most useful. From Italy to Canada, English (or equivalent), mathematics, science, and at least one foreign language and one humanity/social science are studied until 16 by all students. In Armenia every child over the age of 6 will be required to learn chess for two hours a week in order, according to the Education Ministry, 'to foster schoolchildren's intellectual development'. There is also an emphasis on the individual's responsibility to learn in order to progress and shape their own future.

Raising academic standards in our education system is necessary if we are to reverse the culture of low aspiration. Every school should be teaching and entering their pupils for qualifications that count. Sadly, this has not been the case. Students at comprehensive schools are now seven times more likely to be entered for an A-Level in media studies. They are half as likely to be entered for

A-Level mathematics as their privately educated peers. As a result there has been a widening gap in the performance between pupils in independent schools and the state sector.

The requirement to study only English and mathematics until sixteen is almost unique to Britain among developed countries and it is dragging our country's educational performance down. In France students at sixteen are examined in mathematics, science, French, history, geography and foreign language, while in Germany the examinable core consists of mathematics, science, German and a foreign language. In the USA mathematics, science, English and history all form part of the core curriculum until sixteen. In Canada, mathematics, science, English, history and languages are all studied until sixteen. In almost every other developed country specialisation does not take place until post sixteen.

In Britain, there are certain subjects which should be part of every pupil's education which remain largely absent from the curriculum for many. For example, the number of pupils taking a modern foreign language has slumped since it was removed as a requirement for Key Stage 4, from 79 per cent in 2000 to 44 per cent today. Meanwhile, the latest figures show that only 24 per cent of those on free school meals were entered for the subject. The same is true with history. We are the only country apart from Albania which does not make some form of national history compulsory until sixteen.

The number of pupils taking History GCSE at comprehensive schoolshas dipped to 30 per cent but when the figures are looked at in closer detail, a similar pattern emerges to languages. Only 18 per cent of students eligible for free school meals entered for the subjects and there is great regional variation. While just 17 per cent of pupils in the Merseyside borough of Knowsley took History GCSE, over 45 per cent of pupils in Richmond did so. Likewise, there are more than half a dozen local authorities including Islington and Rochdale where fewer than 4 per cent of pupils studied the three sciences separately.

Every pupil in every school in the country should be studying rigorous subjects which form the basis of a general education. Alberta is Canada's top performing province according to the OECD's PISA study of international standards, narrowly behind the Asian countries that top the table. It states in its 2010/11 annual report into education that 'a solid grounding in the core subjects of mathematics, language arts, science and social studies is essential for a solid basic education'. To suggest otherwise, to suggest that those from more deprived backgrounds 'can't do' academic study or master the basics of what should be a rounded curriculum, is to condemn a whole swathe of the population to a second-rate education.

With the introduction of the English Baccalaureate (EBACC), the government has begun to tackle this. It is a welcome development, but we must go further. Every pupil should study English, maths, the three separate sciences, a modern foreign language and history/geography until sixteen. Reporting results on a points and part achievement basis would help achieve this and answer the recent criticism of the Education Select Committee that there would be too much focus on the pupils on the margin of gaining a full Baccalaureate.

For technical schools, such as the University Technical Colleges, the core general education would be supplemented with additional technical subjects. Other schools may wish to offer further academic or arts disciplines.

The baccalaureate concept should also be extended to A-Level with an ABacc introduced that is a grouping of top A-Levels. By appearing in league tables this would encourage schools to produce 'Russell Group ready' students rather than trying to maximise A grades in subjects that are not as well regarded as other disciplines. This would provide much better empirical evidence about how many pupils emerging from state schools are academically prepared to go to the top universities. Though not compulsory the ABacc would provide a 'college track' for students from deprived background to gain entry to our top universities.

The ABacc would be a selection of three of the core academic subjects of mathematics, the sciences, English, foreign languages, history and geography. A minimum of AS mathematics and an AS in history, English or a modern language should be included in the measure. For those studying 3.5-4 A Levels, a further AS or A-Level could be taken.

Introducing an ABacc would help provide the brightest students with a clear route through the system. Currently only 15 per cent of students at comprehensive schools were entered for three of the Russell Group set of 'facilitating', i.e. preferred, A levels compared to 30 per cent of their privately educated peers. This difference becomes even more pronounced when looking at the top performers – 20 per cent of privately educated students gained AAB or above in three 'facilitating' subjects compared to only 6 per cent at comprehensive schools. As with GCSEs there is significant variation between regions. In Knowsley, only 1 per cent of state educated students were entered for three 'facilitating' subjects compared to 25 per cent in Hammersmith and Fulham.

Such a measure would provide increased transparency to students about what universities consider to be high value subjects. It would also provide greater breadth by asking those specialising in science to 'elect' a humanity and those studying arts to 'elect' a science, while preserving the advantage of the depth of the English system.

We also need strong alternatives to the ABacc offering technological and arts options for 16–18 year olds. These would have the support of leading employers or further education institutions to demonstrate that they commanded real world value. These could be developed from existing BTEC Nationals and would also include English and Mathematics. While specialisation often begins at sixteen, students abroad normally continue the study of mathematics and their own language. In its recent paper on mathematics at post-sixteen the Nuffield Foundation called Britain an outlier among competitor countries in having the lowest post-sixteen participation rate.

England, Scotland, Wales and Northern Ireland are four of only six countries out of those Nuffield surveyed that do not require compulsory participation in mathematics at post-sixteen for any students. The 2011 Wolf Report reviewing vocational education found that Britain was 'effectively unique' in lacking a requirement for all students in post-sixteen education to continue studying mathematics and their own language.

At the same time there should be a cull of those qualifications that do not satisfy employers or universities. The government should stop funding, for example, the Travel and Tourism A-Level, which commands little value in the employment market.

Increasing responsibility in education

To support the achievement of higher standards, Britain should adopt the 'escalator' principle which has been successful in improving school systems in Canada and Germany. Students should be expected to reach a minimum standard before progressing to the next academic year while the most able should be allowed to accelerate through the system. For example twin mathematics GCSEs will shortly be introduced, currently titled Methods of Mathematics and Applications of Mathematics. These could be rearranged as Mathematics and Additional Mathematics; accelerated students could take both GCSEs with others just studying one. This will guarantee that all students receive a core general education while stretching the most able. It would also put more responsibility onto the student for their own motivation. This has been lacking in Britain for too long.

British political debate often treats the problems in education as being about the background of the student, rather than the school or the teacher. If only the school had a more 'mixed catchment' it would do better is the thought. There is an underlying assumption that the background of the pupil will have the most impact on their education. In fact the quality of the teaching is the most important factor; and in England those teaching poorer students are often less qualified than those teaching richer students, particularly in core subjects like mathematics.

Teaching has a major workforce problem; it is heavily unionised and has restrictive terms and conditions, which should be unacceptable in a modern profession. Teachers are paid a third of what doctors receive and those in quantitative subjects are much worse paid than accountants or bankers.

We are now reaping the results of the education failures introduced in the 1960s and 1970s as poorly educated teachers enter the workforce, especially in subjects which have the greatest shortages (for example, in mathematics which has the largest number of vacancies). Thus we have the primary school class drilled on multiplication by calculator because the teachers themselves cannot do basic arithmetic.

Attempts to change the system have focused on top down performance measurement. The belief that everything can be reduced to measurement has pervaded the system, and this has reduced the role for judgement and discretion. Teachers are measured by so called 'objective' criteria rather than the judgement of their line manager, removing authority from senior staff. No successful businesses assess their team purely in this way.

There is also a strong culture of denial about the state of education. People who recognise failures in the education establishment are scared of speaking out. For example Katharine Birbalsingh, a vice principal at a Southwark comprehensive, ended up resigning her post due to pressure from staff and governors after she publicly criticised the current situation.

We should be less timid in challenging these entrenched structures. No-one actively voted for our schools to be dominated by skills at the expense of knowledge and a series of subjects with ever decreasing academic credibility. The views of a powerful and organised minority have shaped the system in a way that has damaged the country. It is time that the majority fought back. The academy and free school agenda and curriculum review is moving in the right direction. Reform however needs to be more radical if we are to catch up the international educational leaders.

It is shameful that so many young people have been missold qualifications that will deliver negligible value in their future lives. The state should not pay for such courses. If someone wants to study media studies or law (at a pre-university level), they should pay for it themselves. If the government restricted funding to courses such as English, mathematics, languages, sciences, history and geography there would be more resources to be spent on recruiting top quality teachers.

Teaching desperately needs to raise its prestige and attract new people into the profession. This will not be done by feel good adverts but by raising the financial rewards and capacity for professional judgement of teachers. Teaching is a profession; there is no need for national pay bargaining. Good teachers should be paid more and poor ones should be sacked. According to the General Teaching Council, just eighteen teachers have ever been dismissed for professional incompetence in the past forty years. In no walk of life in the private sector, could that hold true. No-one wants to dismiss any teachers, but without the ability to reward good performers and let go those who are failing, everyone suffers – especially our children. Schools should publish qualifications of teachers on their websites and that would become a key judgement in school choice. Schools should be run much more like professional services companies with peer review, decent line management, an open culture and proper in house training and development.

The current government has made a good start in reforming education, but in order to remain competitive in the future we will have to go further. Our school system must be opened up, our teachers given their independence back, and our pupils more responsibility for their own learning. Only then are we likely to stop our current sad decline in the world rankings. Our children deserve no less.

SUMMARY AGENDA

- We should expand the current free school programme, allowing such schools to make a profit.
- A core general education including maths, science, English, history and languages should be compulsory up to age sixteen. An ABacc should be developed to provide a 'college track' for bright students from all backgrounds with a strong technical alternative.
- We should seek to end grade inflation through the creation of a single examination board 'owned' by the top universities.
- Students failing to achieve the required level should be 'held back' a year. Fast progressing students should be accelerated through school courses.
- We should give schools more powers to dismiss failing teachers and reward better their strongest performers.

SECTION TWO

HOME AND ABROAD

8. British Justice: Firm but Fair

Restoring public confidence in the criminal justice system

Prison and sentencing policy should enjoy public confidence. This can only be achieved by putting victims and public safety first. Public confidence in the criminal justice system is now at sufficiently low level to cause significant concern. To many Britons, our criminal justice system simply isn't working.

Statistics from the Ministry of Justice draw a picture of a justice system that protects offenders and defendants but often fails the victims of crime. Many persistent offenders are only sent to prison after committing dozens – and in some cases hundreds – of crimes. It is striking that 79 per cent of people are confident that the criminal justice system respects the rights of the accused and treats them fairly, but as many as 56 per cent of people are not confident in the system's ability to bring criminals to justice.[127]

---

127   Dominic Smith, Ministry of Justice Research Series 16/10, 'Public confidence in the Criminal Justice System: findings from the British Crime Survey 2002/03 to 2007/08', July 2010, pg 6, http://www.justice.gov.uk/downloads/publications/research-and-analysis/moj-research/confidence-cjs-british-crime-survey.pdf

Lenient sentencing is often aggravated by early release requirements. Those offenders who do end up behind bars are frequently let out far too early. Most violent offenders are let out within a year, and over half of all rapists are back on our streets within eight years. Around half of adults released from prison and three-quarters of young people from youth custody reoffend within a year.[128]

Put simply, there is a perception that punishments are nowhere close to fitting the seriousness of the crimes committed. The public is becoming increasingly frustrated with human rights excuses being deployed by lawyers to keep criminals out of prison and to stop authorities from deporting foreign criminals from the UK.

Despite the protestations of politicians and the legal profession, the public remains sceptical about the efficiency of the justice system. 62 per cent of people are not very confident or not confident at all in the effectiveness of the justice system at reducing crime. 58 per cent think the justice system does not deal with cases promptly and efficiently. Only 65 per cent are confident that the justice system meets the needs of the victims of crime.[129]

In the long term the only means of restoring the people's faith in the system is by reflecting the public's

---

128 Ministry of Justice, 'Breaking the Cycle: Effective Punishment, Rehabilitation and Sentencing of Offenders', 2010

129 Dominic Smith, Ministry of Justice Research Series 16/10, 'Public confidence in the Criminal Justice System: findings from the British Crime Survey 2002/03 to 2007/08', July 2010, pg 6, http://www.justice.gov.uk/downloads/publications/research-and-analysis/moj-research/confidence-cjs-british-crime-survey.pdf

values in our sentencing and the operation of our prisons. As a responsible and liberal society, we should clearly give our citizens the widest possible freedom as long as they operate within the law. When the law is broken, our condemnation should be unequivocal. The primary purpose of our justice system is to protect our society, not to act as a welfare service for convicted criminals.

Soft justice and human rights

In recent years, there has been a surge of soft justice, placing more value on the rights of offenders than those of victims.

Prolific criminals with multiple offences often avoid being sent to jail for their crimes and are instead given feeble community sentences. There are substantial discounts for guilty pleas. Mandatory releases midway through the determinate sentences are handed down by the courts and other early release schemes are putting dangerous criminals back onto our streets.

Consider the facts. Over 10,000 violent offenders were released from prison having served less than one year in prison in 2010. Eighty-six rapists were set free before reaching the halfway point in their sentence in 2010; one-third of violent offenders released in 2010, over 6,500 criminals, were also set free having served less than half of their sentence.

Since a large number of criminals are released, it is hardly surprising to see a prolific rate of reoffending among them. In 2010, 224 rapists who were free on licence were recalled for committing further offences. This figure compares with 763 rapists released from jail that year. The figures for other serious offenders are just as alarming. Over 3,200 violent offenders were recalled in 2010 along with more than 500 sex offenders after receiving further convictions while free on licence.

Some judges have declined to jail criminals on human rights grounds. They say that jail could adversely affect the private life of the offender. In other cases criminals obtain a get out of jail free card in exchange for mere promises of good behaviour. Many of our constituents are puzzled by such supposed human rights as the 'right' to start a family from prison through artificial insemination.

Britain appears to have reached a point where judges are almost apologetic to criminals for having to send them to prison. In one case in Essex, a persistent offender responsible for over 600 crimes was rewarded for his bad behaviour with a home to live in with his girlfriend. Obliviously it was paid for by the taxpayer. While his victims were left feeling thoroughly dissatisfied, he was free to commit more crimes on what effectively became a taxpayer subsidised crime spree. In another case a judge let a paedophile caught downloading child pornography walk free because of an edict from the then Home Secretary dissuading judges from sending people to prison.[130]

A justice system that allows criminals to escape punishment for their crimes is not only disrespectful to the victims of crime. It is also deeply damaging to society by discouraging personal responsibility. Get out of jail free cards should be confined to the Monopoly board.

We need to reverse the tide of soft justice. Prison should be both tougher and more effective.

---

130   http://www.metro.co.uk/news/34736-child-porn-man-freed-by-reids-new-rule

Prison works

As an institution, prison works on many levels. Most fundamentally it protects the wider public by keeping criminals locked up securely. Violent criminals cannot commit further offences while they are in prison. For this reason alone, prison must always remain an integral part of the justice system and a tool that judges should not be shy about using.

However, prison must also go further. As well as protecting the public, prison should punish criminals. It should act both as a deterrent and rehabilitate offenders for their return to the community. Our current high reoffending rates clearly demonstrate that current prison policy is failing to punish, deter and rehabilitate in a satisfactory manner.

Punishment in the justice system is too often a dirty word. The ever increasing human rights agenda and increasing interference from Europe discourage prison sentences. There is a belief that prisoners should be treated in prison in a way that reflects the normal life of freedom that all citizens generally enjoy.[131]

We are not ashamed to say that prisons should be tough, unpleasant and uncomfortable places. That's the point of them. Once an offender has gone to prison they should not want to return. It is concerning that many persistent offenders regard prison sentences as little more

---

131   For example, 'Promoting alternatives to imprisonment' (Document 12659 from the Parliamentary Assembly for the Council of Europe, 22 June 2011); 'European Prison Rules (Recommendation No. R (87)3 Council of Europe)'; and 'Recommendation No. R (2003)23 of the Committee of Ministers to member States on the management by prison administrations of life sentence and other long-term prisoners.'

than an opportunity for 'respite' or to 'chill out' rather than as a deterrent.[132] Strict regimes, including work activities, must be enforced to promote some measure of discipline.

It has been argued in the past that instead of short prison sentences, there should be a presumption against sending criminals to prison. This is the wrong approach to take. We should take exactly the opposite approach and ensure that persistent offenders are imprisoned for prolonged periods of time. Not only would these longer prison sentences keep the public safe, they would also give offenders a genuine opportunity to be rehabilitated.

Interestingly, research from the Howard League for Penal Reform has highlighted, from the perspective of the offender, some of the failings with short sentences of less than one year. This is particularly relevant in the case of repeat offenders. In terms of rehabilitation, the research showed that short term prisoners complained that 'offending behaviour courses and jobs were difficult to come by and often given to prisoners serving longer sentences'. Long waiting lists and a lack of availability of relevant courses were also cited as barriers for short term prisoners, which also prevented prisoners from completing courses during their sentences.[133]

Longer and tougher prison sentences
Prisoners spending more time in prison could be placed on longer courses and training programmes to reform

---

132 The Howard League for Penal Reform, 'No winners: the reality of short term prison sentences,' 2011, pg 24.

133 The Howard League for Penal Reform, 'No winners: the reality of short term prison sentences,' 2011, pg 19 & pp.23–4.

their behaviour and obtain qualifications to help them turn their lives around. At the moment, the justice system is delivering poor value for money on education and training courses. Only around half of all prisoners on a course complete their targets. While there is a shortage of opportunities for prisoners requiring basic education and training needs, the justice system is still able to provide degree level courses to some 1,600 prisoners. Resources should be ploughed into supporting education and rehabilitation at a more basic and fundamental level.

More generally, there is a strong correlation between longer prison sentences and lower reoffending rates. Research found that offenders who had served a sentence of less than one year had a reoffending frequency rate (the number of offences per 100 offenders) of 308.4 compared to a reoffending frequency rate of 46.8 among offenders with a sentence length of four years or more.[134] People who stay in prison longer are, statistically, less likely to reoffend.

Longer sentences would also mean that public, private and third sector service providers would have more time to work with offenders to address underlying issues, such as addiction and illiteracy. By paying providers for results and outcomes rather than methods, we can allow them to experiment and improve efficiency. The same discipline should be extended to all community sentences and efficiencies could be achieved by those operating prison based programmes also operating those outside.

It is essential that the private sector and independent organisations are brought in to provide rehabilitation

---

134 Ministry of Justice Statistics bulletin, 'Reoffending of adults: results from the 2008 cohort', March 2010, pg 21

services. The monolithic approach of the public sector, as applied by the National Offender Management Service (NOMS), has failed to tackle reoffending. By adopting similar methods to those used to reduce unemployment through the Work Programme, these companies and organisations will be able to introduce a wave of innovation and improvement in the justice system.

Project Barbed at HMP Coldingley is a good illustration of the kind of scheme that must be made to work. Prisoners worked in a graphic design studio, acquiring skills and engaging in productive work that would prepare them for life on release. The project was closed down under the last government, principally because of the stifling bureaucracy and inflexibility in our prisons. Expanding work in prisons would also help fund victim compensation, from prisoner earnings, an important component of restorative justice.

In addition to work and training, far greater emphasis must be placed on addressing alcohol and drug addiction in our prisons. It is a sad fact that many offenders become addicts for the first time when they are incarcerated, because UK prisons are awash with drugs. Drug and alcohol rehabilitation must be a central focus of a more purposeful prison regime. Under the last government, drug addicts were too often left to languish on methadone prescriptions that sought to stabilise, but not cure, their addiction. This defeatist attitude must be changed. It hurts the prisoner and harms society. A far greater emphasis must be placed on abstinence-based rehabilitation, with personalised plans that are designed to get offenders off all drug and alcohol dependencies.

The system currently often fails all parties. Victims of crime and the wider public perceive prison regimes as soft and an inadequate punishment. Victims feel the system is against them and on the side of the law breakers. Longer prison sentences would increase confidence in the system, help cut reoffending, and improve public safety.

Affording reform

Reforming this situation will not be easy. The coalition inherited an impoverished system: overcrowded prisons, little new capacity coming on stream and no money to rectify the shortfall. In the near-term, Britain will need more cells in order to re-establish prison both as an effective deterrent and a more constructive place of rehabilitation.

There is some potential to free up space. Our prisons are filled with over 10,000 foreign national criminals. Likewise, the last government steadily reduced the number of secure NHS places for the mentally ill, who now often end up in prison. The NHS should take responsibility for the significant proportion of prisoners who are seriously mentally ill.

Britain's prisons could also be much more cost effective – currently they cost £45,000 per place per year. This is far higher than other countries such as the US and European counterparts, where places cost below £30,000. All the evidence suggests that prisons in the private sector are 15 per cent cheaper and also achieve more in getting prisoners working. The government should contract out the remaining public sector prisons and break the hegemony of the Prison Officers Association.

Britain has one of the most expensive criminal justice systems in the world with a high rate of reoffending. Currently Community Payback (one type of community sentence) is contracted out on a pan-regional basis, prisons are run on a national basis and probation trusts are run locally. Although there is theoretically a National Offender Management Service, in practice there are different fiefdoms with alternative cultures. The crucial link between police and probation has been weakened by the separation between the Ministry of Justice and the Home Office under the previous government. There is not a strong enough focus throughout the organisation on reducing reoffending.

The government should extend the role of Police Commissioner to a Police and Justice Commissioner and make them responsible for commissioning sentences for those who are convicted. These sentences could include custodial and non-custodial elements including tagging post release to minimise the risk of reoffending. A single contractor could be awarded the full service provision, thus breaking the split between custodial and non-custodial sentences. Those responsible for running work in prisons would also be responsible for running community service outside, and the regime under which the offender was placed would be similarly tough. Once an offender had left prison, the same provider would be responsible for preventing them from reoffending for a given period afterwards (for example ten years).

Contractors would be rewarded on a payment by results basis so that there would be a clear incentive to reduce reoffending. Judges and magistrates should be supplied with evidence on the efficacy of these punishments so that they can make the best judgements about what works. Contracting out more prison places would reduce the very high costs of British prisons in comparison to those overseas and create competition about how effectively the prison worked.

Once these reforms were in place, Britain would have both a more efficient and a more effective prison system.

Such a system would be better placed to handle the longer prison sentences our justice system badly needs, and once again regain the public's confidence.

Immigration: rebuilding a generation betrayed

Before the 2010 general election, it was a subject that no party wished to talk about. Gillian Duffy's encounter with Gordon Brown on the streets of Rochdale changed that. In branding her a 'bigoted woman', Brown himself explained better than anyone else how Labour had lost touch with the working population of Britain.

The Conservative Party believed that everyone understood its immigration policy. The truth was that few people felt that any party was listening to their concerns. The simple figures explain why their voices, clearly expressed on any doorstep across the country, should have been heard long before. There has been a visible shift in the demographic pattern of employment, away from UK nationals, towards migrants gaining full-time employment in the UK. While the total working population of the UK has only slightly increased from 28.2 million in 1997 to 29.1 million in 2011, the number of non-UK/non-EU nationals working in the country has risen from 501,000 to 1,193,000, with the number of EU nationals rising from 216,000 to 1,308,000.[135] At the same time, the percentage of UK nationals in full-time employment has dropped from 51 per cent to 47 per cent. Even these figures remain difficult to analyse given that around 1.5 million migrant workers have acquired British nationality since 1997.

---

135   http://www.publications.parliament.uk/pa/cm201011/cmhansrd/cm110712/text/110712w0002.htm

Statistics may point to the problem, but public attitudes and feeling towards immigration cut far deeper. At the centre is the issue of fairness: we must understand that the British public feel a strong sense of betrayal towards the previous Labour government, who presided over an unprecedented level of immigration without any control. In growing the economy on the back of non-UK labour, and in allowing the EU expansion to take place without necessary controls over the flow of free labour, New Labour placed additional pressure on a generation of UK workers. We must rebuild the confidence and motivation of the UK working population.

We want Britain to be an enterprise nation, one which is able to compete for international business, vital to ensure growth and economic recovery. Yet that recovery will be a false one if it is not grounded upon a national labour market that has the skills to compete. We need the brightest and the best to invest in the UK, but we also want to ensure that UK nationals are those brightest and best. This will be a long process, but one which must better link education to the jobs that employers need.

We need to also recognise that there is a crucial difference between coming here to work, for a set period, and then to be almost automatically offered citizenship. British citizenship is all too easily assigned, and in consequence is taken for granted. This must change, with the link between migration and citizenship removed. Instead, we should look to create a means by which citizenship is a privilege to be earned.

The use of green cards is well established in the USA. Although it does not give the holder full citizenship, a green card allows the holder to live and work in the United States. It allows the holder to be a lawful permanent resident who pays tax, to travel abroad and re-enter the country. It does not, however, give automatic citizenship rights, which can only be applied for after several years. There are strict quota limits, also set at different levels for different countries, and family migration is also strictly controlled. For example, the spouse of a US citizen could be granted a green card immediately, whereas the brother or sister of that citizen might have to wait ten years or more. Green cards provide a recognition that citizenship is not an automatic right that can simply be applied for, but rather a journey, during along which applicants must prove their contribution to civic society, both in terms of employment but also towards their neighbourhood and local community.

In the UK, automatic rights of citizenship include access to benefits, something which EU workers are also entitled to after a certain number of years of employment. Currently the link between migration and citizenship is too close and needs to be broken with a graduated approach. The introduction of 'Enterprise cards', along similar lines to a US green card would allow for strict quota limits for non-EU workers to be set. The criteria for this Enterprise card would need to be developed. One possibility might be for each migrant worker, upon entry to the UK to be given an Enterprise card. There would be automatic recognition that no worker would be entitled to state benefits, schooling, or NHS services, without advance payment. Only after 10 years would an Enterprise card holder be eligible for UK citizenship, having demonstrated employment and a record of paying tax over ten years.

SUMMARY AGENDA

- We should restore public confidence in the justice system by seeking longer, tougher prison sentences. These would not only better protect the public but give the offender more opportunity for rehabilitation.
- A robust policy of transferring and deporting foreign national prisoners, coupled with the transfer of the mentally ill to secure hospitals, would ease pressure on the prison estate and free up places for serious and persistent criminal offenders.
- The remainder of England's prisons should be contracted out to the private sector on a payments by results basis, reducing the bills for prisons by at least 15 per cent.
- The prison regime needs to be overhauled, so that our jails are not simply human warehouses, but constructive regimes that promote work, training and alcohol and drug rehabilitation.
- We should create new 'Enterprise cards', setting strict quota limits on the immigration of both EU and non-EU workers.

9. Justice and Liberty: Defending British Rights

'**I** know what you're saying about protecting our liberties. But then I look at my five year old daughter, and I'm just not willing to take the risk.' So said a prominent British neo-conservative, in one of Parliament's many debates on proposals to extend pre-charge detention. Yet, if we follow that logic, Britain will cease to be the kind of free country that we want our children to grow up in. In twenty-first century Britain, we have allowed our apathy to prevail. We have acquiesced in the gradual emasculation of our liberty. It is not just our freedoms that we are sacrificing. Over the past decade, we seem to have forgotten some of the values that define what it means to be British, such as liberty, democratic accountability and meritocracy.

Ever since Alfred the Great first translated the word *libertas* into English, this country has identified individual freedom with a corresponding measure of personal responsibility. Our liberty was born of free choice – and that meant bearing the consequences of our actions.

The British tradition preserved a finite list of basic freedoms from interference, abuse or mistreatment by the state, from the ancient right of habeas corpus, and the right to trial by jury and to freedom of speech. Over time, these fundamental rights have been gradually eroded. Draconian counter-terrorism legislation has extended pre-charge detention to the longest period in the free world; it has imposed virtual house arrest on individuals not yet convicted of any crime. ASBOs have been dished out to truculent youths and even to an eccentric English evangelist preaching 'Be a winner with Jesus' on a soap box on Oxford Street. Meanwhile, local council snoopers in Poole followed children home from school to verify their catchment area, despite no information to suggest their parents lied. Other officers in Cambridge followed paperboys to check the licences of newsagents. It is a sign of the times that paper boys even need licences – let alone that precious taxpayers' money is being wasted on monitoring them.

None of these intrusions will make us safer. Evidence shows police need a fraction of the ninety days pre-charge detention proposed by Tony Blair. Control orders leak like a sieve. ASBOs are regarded as a badge of honour by yobs. Council tax squandered on petty surveillance wastes precious law enforcement resources.

2010 saw another disreputable first, as a criminal trial was held without a jury for the first time in 400 years. Armed robbers accused of theft from a warehouse in Heathrow then tried to corrupt jury members, disrupting two trials at immense cost to the taxpayer. Rather than paying the £6 million necessary for proper jury protection, the authorities allowed three trials to collapse – at a cost of over £20million – and then abandoned the jury. This is the worst of all worlds.

The coalition has made substantial strides to tackle some of Labour's most illiberal legacy. They have abolished ID cards, halved pre-charge detention and restricted stop-and-search powers. It has also made a commitment to defend the principle of trial by jury. However, these important initiatives mark a point of departure, not arrival.

For example, the new Terrorism Prevention and Investigation Measures (TPIMs) are not as draconian as control orders. But the potential restrictions remain serious. They include residency requirements, curfews, limits on communication and association, travel bans and electronic tagging. They still undermine a key principle of British justice: that a defendant should be presumed innocent until proven guilty. In one important respect TPIMs are worse than what went before. Control orders had to be approved annually by Parliament in recognition of their exceptional nature and the urgency of the circumstances in which they were introduced. This ensured regular parliamentary oversight. However, TPIMs will not be subject to such parliamentary reviews. A temporary emergency measure has now become permanent and entrenched.

This is particularly regrettable, since there are other ways to reconcile freedom and security. For example, Britain needs a more robust prosecution policy, drawing on lessons abroad, especially in the United States, Australia and Canada. There should be greater tactical use of plea bargaining to secure convictions, as practised extensively in America. If this technique were deployed effectively, it would almost certainly increase, not reduce, the number of dangerous people put behind bars.

Government ministers should also overcome bureaucratic inertia to lift the ban on the use of intercept evidence in court. This would end Britain's virtual global isolation on this issue. Intercept evidence is a useful tool for prosecuting terrorist. Given that the number of terrorists sent to jail has plummeted by 90 per cent in the last four years, despite the persistence of the threat from them, there is an urgent need for a rethink. In that way, we can start using the justice system as a weapon in the fight against terror, rather than viewing it as an impediment to effective law enforcement.

Equally, the assault on liberty was not only the fault of the last government. The subtle erosion of free speech stems in part from the Public Order Act 1986, exacerbated by its poor interpretation by the police and the Crown Prosecution Service.

Section 5 of the Public Order Act rightly outlaws words and behaviour which are threatening violence or which constitute tangible abuse. But, it also criminalises those who are merely insulting. There are numerous examples of how this has led to arrests and prosecutions, like the fifteen-year-old boy served with a summons for holding a placard at a demonstration calling the Church of Scientology a 'cult'. The charges were later dropped, but only after the police had interfered with a peaceful and legitimate protest.

In an even more serious case in 2009, hotel owners Ben and Sharon Vogelenzang were dragged to court after a guest was upset by a discussion about religion. A Muslim guest told them that Jesus was a minor prophet, and that the Bible is not true. In reply, Mrs Vogelenzang said that she could not understand why Muslim women wearing Islamic dress would put themselves into bondage. On that basis, they were prosecuted, going through the trauma of going to trial. The judge eventually threw the case out, but their business was badly affected by the prosecution and closed in September 2010.

The Vogelenzang case highlights two points. Firstly, the damaging impact the current law has on free speech.

Secondly, the arbitrary decision of the police taking the hotel managers, but not the guest, to task. Neither party should have been charged for a heated debate about religion, but it is difficult to understand why the police deemed one set of comments more insulting than the other. And this is the problem. What one person finds offensive, another takes in his stride. The sheer breadth of section 5, with its highly subjective concept of people being 'insulted', lays it wide open to abuse. John Stuart Mill famously argued that 'the only purpose for which power can rightfully be exercised over any member of a civilised community, against his will .... is to prevent harm to others' – tangible harm, not mere offence. That is the only reason to ban free speech. The Public Order Act should be amended accordingly.

The irony is that, while free speech is being stifled, too often the police have been prepared to indulge those preaching violence. In 2006, there were angry protests against the publication of Danish cartoons of the Prophet Mohammed. A number of people carried placards with slogans calling on Muslims to 'bomb' the US and Denmark and 'butcher those who insult Islam'. Four protestors were eventually convicted of soliciting murder. However, the Metropolitan Police did not interfere with the protest at the time for fear of public disorder. This was an astonishing capitulation to extremism. It took six weeks before any arrests were made.

Likewise, it took the authorities years to tackle extremist preacher Abu Hamza, who had been making hate-filled speeches at Finsbury Park mosque since 1997, but was not arrested until 2004. He openly encouraged violence against Jews and other non-Muslims, but it took a US extradition request to bring him to justice.

The authorities must take an uncompromising

approach to those inciting violence. The government's new PREVENT strategy represents an encouraging shift of emphasis. Britain should not be throwing taxpayer's money at those who don't support the values of a tolerant and democratic society. But, nor should we be wrapping our society in cotton wool, to try and prevent everyone and anyone from suffering mere offence from free debate in a vibrant democracy. The balance of law needs to be redressed in favour of free speech and our wider freedoms.

Elsewhere, over-zealous prosecutors, Whitehall bureaucrats and jobsworth local officials have been joined by the European Union in eroding the British tradition of freedom. Progressive Europhiles have struggled to reconcile their instinctive support for Europe with its increasingly illiberal expansion into justice and home affairs. Dogmatic commitment to EU integration should not be allowed to supersede traditional British liberties.

The most obvious illustration is fast track extradition under the European Arrest Warrant (EAW). It has led to numerous injustices, like the detention of Andrew Symeou, whisked away to a hot Greek jail crawling with cockroaches, for alleged involvement in a nightclub fight that led to a tragic death, despite eye witness accounts that he was never there. Mr Symeou spent almost a year in appalling conditions before being released on bail. During this time, he was abused by guards and witnessed another prisoner being beaten to death. At the time of writing, his trial was proceeding at a snail's pace, hampered by translators who speak little English.

The EAW licences the most Kafkaesque of practices. Deborah Dark, a grandmother of two, was acquitted of drug offences in France in 1989. Unbeknown to her, French prosecutors appealed and she was sentenced to two years imprisonment in her absence. Seventeen years later, on holiday in Turkey, she was arrested at gunpoint. It took three years for the case to be dropped.

Such cases are becoming all too common. The number of British citizens surrendered to European authorities under EAWs has risen from two a month (in 2004) to two a day. For every warrant the UK issues today, we receive twenty back. While less frequently abused, UK–US extradition relations are also unbalanced given the different evidential thresholds for extradition.

UK extradition arrangements should be reformed – with both the EU and US. The liberty of the British citizen should not be sacrificed for diplomatic convenience or expediency.

The Human Rights Act has proved a flimsy shield against these attacks on our freedoms, whether they arise from authoritarian legislation, operational abuse or the EU. The coalition has made a series of improvements, most notably through repealing various items of the last government's legislation in its Protection of Freedoms Bill. However, such reforms should be protected by the adoption of a British Bill of Rights, steeped in our history and tailored to modern needs. We should remain committed to defending the citizen against an increasingly clumsy and arbitrary state.

Liberty is a fundamental pillar in our democracy. But, it is not the only one. British liberal democracy is also based on the rule of law and democratic accountability. This has been expressed historically through the concept of Parliamentary sovereignty. The development of new human rights, from a finite list of core freedoms to the whole area of economic, social and now even environmental human rights raises a range of important questions. They should be debated and determined by lawmakers elected by and accountable to the British public.

Instead, they have been developed by the courts – both the European Court of Human Rights in Strasbourg and, especially since the Human Rights Act, the UK courts – which are without democratic debate or control.

Judges have used the general wording of the European Convention on Human Rights to overrule the UK law of negligence as it applies to the police. At the same time they have told parents how to discipline their children. They have elevated welfare and social entitlements to constitutionally enforceable human rights. They have managed to undermine free speech in favour of an all-conquering right to privacy.

In a ground-breaking decision in 2005, the Strasbourg Court ordered Britain to give prisoners the vote, a novel right conjured out of thin air and in defiance of the terms of European Convention. More worrying, it has expanded the scope of various rights to frustrate deportation orders against convicted criminals and terrorist suspects. In one case, a man convicted of killing a young waiter and dumping his body in the river Thames escaped deportation back to Nepal by claiming a right to family life even though he has no dependants in the UK. The ruling was delivered in direct conflict with the express terms of Article 8 of the European Convention, which expressly allows action to protect the public, enforce the law or prevent crime. Some of these developments have outraged a bewildered public.

Other recent cases include a Sri Lankan robber allowed to remain in the country because he has a girlfriend here (the court described the relationship as 'casual courting') and a Trinidadian drug offender who, despite beating his girlfriend and avoiding maintenance payments for his daughter, escaped deportation to the Caribbean because of Article 8. This development has been criticised by Lord Carlile, the former independent reviewer of Britain's anti-terror laws, who has complained that 'a narrow interpretation of the Convention has had a chilling effect on deportation and thereby on public safety'.

The full scale of the problem caused by this judge-led innovation became apparent in 2011. The release of Home Office statistics showed that around 400 foreign criminals a year are now using Article 8 to avoid deportation. In addition there are also thousands of failed asylum seekers and EU 'benefit tourists'. Article 8 cases now account for 61 per cent of all successful deportation appeals made by foreign criminals.

These cases are symptoms of a wider problem. A British Bill of Rights could not only strengthen our individual freedoms, but also wrest democratic control over the creation of new rights back from the courts. We can then strike a proper balance between individual rights, personal responsibility and the wider public interest.

If government has eroded our liberty and the courts have undermined democratic accountability, the State has also crossed the rubicon from defending equal opportunity to social engineering promoting positive discrimination. The implementation of the 2010 Equality Act has introduced regulations requiring 25,000 schools, police forces, councils and other public bodies to audit their staff according to gender, ethnicity, sexuality, religion and other political beliefs. These bodies must now demonstrate, on an annual basis, how they are promoting diversity through recruitment, policies and practices. This Orwellian intrusion into the privacy of staff is aggravated by the attempt to engineer a more diverse mix of employees in the workplace. There is no proper guidance on what constitutes the right social mix in any given place or profession. Confusing and costly at best, the regulations are a recipe for bitter resentment, not greater diversity.

At the same time, the debate on gender equality has been hijacked by the obsession of the Equality and Human Rights Commission with promoting gender quotas, particularly in the corporate boardroom. Too often, the Commission's agenda belittles the significant progress towards greater female representation. There remain social creases in modern Britain. But gender equality has come a long way. Women in their twenties now earn on average 2 per cent more than men according to the Office for National Statistics. Half the top positions in the Civil Service are occupied by women. While the number of female FTSE 100 executive directors remains too low, the figure has at least doubled since 2000.

Above all, the fixation on boardroom quotas is elitist, ignoring the large number of women on middle incomes, who face no overt discrimination but find their careers fall back amidst the constant struggling and striving to strike the right work–life balance. Anachronistic and anti-meritocratic quotas will not do anything to address this challenge. Rather than harking back to the outdated and divisive battle of the sexes, waged since the 1960s, young couples would benefit more from family-friendly policies to help them strike the right career–family balance, a challenge most couples share and want to tackle together.

Worst of all, the Equality Act has now introduced positive discrimination in the workplace, where several candidates are 'as qualified as each other'. In the Soviet style double-speak of the Equality and Human Rights Commission this is merely 'positive action'. Yet, when it comes to offering a job, the decisive factor may well be race, religion, gender, sexuality, or age. It will be voluntary to begin with, but the Commission clearly expects to encourage its wider application. Positive discrimination warps the basic value of equality. It can lead to double standards and has created bitter resentment wherever it has been tried, mainly in countries grappling with historic injustice or ethnic strife. In South Africa, it has created deep rifts. As one opponent, Professor Alexander at Cape Town University, bluntly observed of recent plans to introduce racial benchmarks in university admissions: 'The government under apartheid did the same and we told them to go to hell.'

From a practical point of view, how will a British business know the right social mix to aim for? Firms will inevitably need some form of benchmarks or quotas. New guidance from the government Equalities Office simply states that 'some information or evidence will be required' to hire on social criteria unrelated to merit, 'but it does not need to be sophisticated statistical data or research'. Firms can compare the social mix of their workplace to the locality, sector or national data – which could all conflict. Alternatively, a decision 'may be obtained ... through discussion with workers or their representatives'. This suggests that firms should ask their existing staff – or union representatives – which minorities are inadequately represented. This is a recipe for disaster, stigmatising new recruits and leaving new social divisions. As Kat Akingbade said when she learned she had been awarded a new job as a Channel 4 TV presenter on grounds of colour: 'Positive discrimination robs an individual of drive and self-motivation; it completely undermines the achievements and abilities of the hard-working and truly gifted.'

A Bill of Rights should ban positive discrimination just as clearly as the negative variety. We need to stand up for a British vision of a meritocratic society, a vision that, in the words of Martin Luther King, judges people on the 'content of their character' – as individuals rather than on account of their race, gender, sexuality or religion.

The expansion of the British state since 1997 has eroded freedom, democratic accountability and meritocracy in this country. A Bill of Rights would provide a modern framework for restoring and reviving those characteristic British values.

The free press and the BBC

There is no more important factor to maintaining our ultimate liberty than a free press. A free press reflects society perhaps as it is rather than as we would have it be: divided, over excitable and obsessed with gossip. Nevertheless, despite its excesses, Britain's press throughout its history has guarded against the inevitable corruptions of high power. By expressing differing opinions from a single government view, a free press gives us all the right to have our say, joining in the national debate.

It has become a cliché to point out that our media landscape is now rapidly changing. Where once it was possible to speak of separate radio, television and newspaper markets, the power of the internet is breaking down any borders between them that once existed. It has become ever easier for individuals and small companies to join the national conversation, as anybody with a mobile phone now in effect carries around with them their own portable television studio. Where once the media was confined by political borders, the internet brings us together into a single global market. Only around 40 per cent of the readership of online newspapers such as *The Guardian* and the *Daily Mail* comes from the UK.[136] New funding models are constantly being dreamed up, experimented with and implemented by newspaper companies desperate to discover sustainable profits. Choice is the new watchword, the audience no longer happy to have their schedule dictated by a central gatekeeper.

In such a liberalised world, the BBC is becoming ever more of a theoretical oddity. To many in other countries, paying an annual tax to own a television is as strange an idea as paying a tax to own a mobile phone. Implemented as a poll tax, the licence fee costs the same for the very rich as the very poor.

To see the strangeness, imagine if the government had followed a similar strategy with regard to newspapers. Each year, every person who could read would be forced a flat fee in return for a state owned newspaper being delivered straight to their door. It is difficult to imagine other newspapers thriving in this environment. To most people, the idea that the government should publish its own newspaper, carefully mixed in with popular entertainment to help the consumption of the news, is absurd and slightly scary.

In past centuries, British democrats and rebels fought for the right to free speech, to publish pamphlets and books giving their own view. In broadcasting however, we seem happy to give up this right. ITV, Channel 4 and Channel 5 are required to produce 'public service broadcasting', programmes that are expected to be socially valuable but financially unprofitable. Other broadcasters

---

136 http://www.guardian.co.uk/media/2010/aug/26/abces-july-2010

such as Sky News are expected to maintain a strictly non-partisan voice. Not only is this strange in itself, but it has created a worrying precedent. In the wake of the phone hacking scandal, some such as former Labour leader Neil Kinnock have already suggested that the requirement for 'neutrality' should be spread to newspapers as well. [137]

In general, there are two views on how one can ensure truth and accuracy in the discourse of a nation, making sure that the news doesn't get distorted by ideological or self-interested agendas. The first view is that the best way to ensure truth is to require anyone who speaks to be non-partisan. This is the model we follow in broadcasting. The second view, by contrast, accepts that disagreement is inevitable, and believes that it is better to conduct this disagreement out in the open. Truth is ensured by the free competition of ideas. This is the model of our press, books, the internet and society at large.

The original justifications for the restrictions placed on broadcasting rested on technological limitations. A technological shortage of radio spectrum meant that there would only ever be room for a very limited number of channels, and so it was thought better not to waste this valuable resource. There was no room for competing viewpoints, only one official line. As it is impossible to stop anyone from listening into a radio broadcast, standard business models didn't seem to work.

The original BBC service restricted its broadcasts until after 7 p.m. so as not to compete with newspapers,[138] but this proved unsustainable during the national emergency

---

137 BBC, Today, Radio 4, 19 July 2011, http://news.bbc.co.uk/today/hi/today/newsid_9542000/9542452.stm

138 http://news.bbc.co.uk/aboutbbcnews/spl/hi/history/noflash/html/1920s.stm

of the 1926 General Strike. Nevertheless, having proved its worth as a central focus for national news, the institution was converted into a new public body under royal charter: the British Broadcasting Corporation.

John Reith, the BBC's first Director General, was under no doubt that Britain could not follow the American way and allow free competition in its broadcasting. If it did, he worried,

> the Christian religion and the Sabbath might not have had the place and protection they had; .... one day in the week clear of jazz and variety and such like.... The BBC might have had to play for safety; prosecute the obviously popular lines; count its clients; study and meet their reactions; curry favour; subordinate itself to the vote.[139]

Later, when the House of Lords debated the introduction of commercial television in 1952, Reith complained, 'Somebody introduced dog-racing into England... Somebody introduced smallpox, bubonic plague and the Black Death. Somebody is minded now to introduce sponsored broadcasting into this country... Need we be ashamed of moral values, or of intellectual and ethical objectives? It is these that are here and now at stake.'[140]

But despite Reith's bitter objections, competition was introduced into British broadcasting: first through ITV, then Sky, and now the whole internet. As technology has

---

139 http://www.bbc.co.uk/historyofthebbc/resources/in-depth/reith_5.shtml

140 http://www.bbc.co.uk/historyofthebbc/resources/in-depth/reith_8.shtml

progressed, the original justifications for monopoly have now long since become irrelevant.

Indeed, the present state of technology makes the current model of public sector broadcasting not just redundant but fundamentally broken. It is impossible now to speak of shortage of spectrum. By contrast, it is perfectly possible to restrict content only to those who have paid. The television as a device is gradually losing its prominence. More and more of us watch programmes instead on our laptop or our mobile. The BBC is no longer just a leading provider of video and audio, but text as well through its bbc.co.uk website. It has created the national newspaper by stealth.

Meanwhile, publications such as *The Guardian* and *The Telegraph* are producing ever more video content, despite their admittedly partisan views. The law no longer makes any sense. Why should News International be required to be perfectly neutral in the videos on its Sky News website but be allowed to declare for a party on *The Times* website?

Clearly, the licence fee in its current form is no longer sustainable. If a similar model is to be continued, it will have to become conditional on something more basic than owning a television. The most likely scenario seems to be that it will eventually have to be charged to anyone who has internet access.

But before we take such a step, it is worth taking the opportunity to look at whether this is really the model we wish for the future of the British media.

The main reason most people defend the BBC is that while a tax on TV may be ludicrous in theory, in practice it seems to work. The BBC, it is claimed, is relatively cheap. It helps strengthen British culture and is a respected institution across the world. We should not seek to break something that already works so well.

But does the BBC work as well as it could?

Perhaps the BBC's greatest strength and its core purpose is as a news organisation. The BBC clearly does try to maintain its neutral stance – but unfortunately, perfect neutrality is always impossible. Every organisation has its own culture, and it is no surprise considering its industry and location that the BBC's is metropolitan and liberal, as freely admitted by its own staff. BBC reporter Andrew Marr has described the institution as having a 'cultural liberal' bias. Former Washington correspondent Justin Webb complained that the BBC was biased against America.[141] Former newsreader Peter Sissons went so far as to claim:

> By far the most popular and widely read newspapers at the BBC are *The Guardian* and *The Independent*... At any given time there is a BBC line on everything of importance... [The] EU is a good thing, but not quite as good as the UN. Soaking the rich is good... And government spending is a good thing, although most BBC people prefer to call it investment, in line with New Labour's terminology... All green and environmental groups are very good things... The Royal Family is a bore. Islam must not be offended at any price, although Christians are fair game because they do nothing about it if they are offended.[142]

---

141   http://www.dailymail.co.uk/news/article-411846/We-biased-admit-stars-BBC-News.html

142   http://www.dailymail.co.uk/news/article-1349506/Left-wing-bias-Its-written-BBCs-DNA-says-Peter-Sissons.html

No one media company can be perfectly neutral. To have a genuinely balanced media, we need diverse institutions. Unfortunately, the BBC perversely makes it harder for such pluralism to exist, undercutting potential competitors with its own offerings. It is no surprise that newspaper groups and local radio have struggled when the public can always access a free alternative.

Of course, this by itself may not be an argument against the BBC. An official source of news might be such an important public good that it should be provided no matter the effect on the competition. The fact that the government offers each child a free school place may make it harder to set up a private school, but that doesn't mean that we should stop providing free education.

Nevertheless, there is clearly a case for restraint. The BBC should be providing the bare minimum to keep its citizens informed, not trying to be a brand on its own. Opinion pieces, magazine style articles and travel guides are inappropriate. Britain would have a healthier media if the BBC tried its best not to act as a competitor destination site. At the time of writing in summer 2011, the BBC news site is offering magazine pieces asking 'Big number: Is 72 the answer to life, the universe – everything?',[143] 'Flan fingers: Why are custard pies used as a protest?'[144] and 'Online odium: How did Rebecca Black turn dislike into fame?'.[145]

Unfortunately, both the justification for, and record of, the BBC's provision of entertainment is much weaker than in news. The BBC shows little innovation in popular

143   http://www.bbc.co.uk/news/magazine-14217443

144   http://www.bbc.co.uk/news/magazine-14218654

145   http://www.bbc.co.uk/news/magazine-14218654

culture. There is really no need for a state body to be paying huge sums for sports rights, foreign television and copycat reality television formats. The BBC's record on high culture is scarcely any better. Its programmes are frequently surpassed by private organisations such as Sky Arts, while British drama as a whole was long ago far surpassed by the US. The only area of programming in which the BBC still remains a world leader is natural history.

It is often argued that the BBC supports the wider British media industry. A state funded media organisation, it is claimed, allows Britain to protect and project its own culture. Left to the private market, British TV would show nothing but American repeats.

But such a defeatist view makes no sense. The costs of television production are coming down all the time, and in any case as the world's sixth largest economy Britain is large enough to support a domestic industry. Indeed, thanks to our language, we do not face the barriers other countries do in selling our film and television abroad.

Britain is a world leader in cultural exports. Our publishers, film studios, and computer games companies have not required state ownership to enjoy continued success. Indeed, it is perfectly possible to argue that the presence of the BBC has held British television back, forcing on it a very parochial culture rather than focusing on the global market.

If we are to keep it sustainable for the long term, the BBC must undergo a long period of reform. Ultimately, the BBC must focus on its own unique advantages. Instead of trying to compete with the wider market, it should be filling in the gaps that the market will not sustain. There is no reason for it to be paying for

Hollywood films and television, expensive sports rights, soaps such as *Eastenders* and *The Archers*, new reality television formats and so on. There is nothing wrong with such programmes – but they do not need the BBC to be created.

It would be better if the BBC consolidated on its core strengths, creating a new 'thin' BBC. The licence fee should gradually shrink in real terms. If this means that the BBC is forced to sell off elements such as Radio One or BBC Two, so much the better. Ratings will almost certainly go down – but high ratings for showing repeats of blockbuster movies has very little to do with the BBC's original mission in any case.

In the long term, our proposal is that a thin BBC would be easier to fund from general taxation. This would be much fairer and more progressive than trying to create a new broadband tax. At the same time, freeing up the restrictions on other commercial broadcasters would help limit the effects of the BBC's current subsidised dominance of the British media.

The BBC has a long and proud history, but in the decades since its inception has drifted away from its original mission. Reith, for all his faults, was right to say that the BBC should focus on informing, educating and entertaining. The third element of that list has for too long been overly dominant.

In its current form, we risk the BBC's endless expansion fatally undermining the rest of Britain's unsubsidised media market. Our free press is far too important to allow that. Instead, we should return the BBC back to its original principles, focusing on only what it can do and what the market cannot support. This 'thin' BBC should be a supplement to our wider media market, not its competitor.

SUMMARY AGENDA

- We should create a Bill of Rights that protects Britain's tradition of liberty, enshrines meritocracy and restores democratic control over the wider human rights agenda.
- We should reform media regulation to preserve freedom of the press and promote media pluralism in the new digital age. A new 'thin BBC' should return it to its original mission to 'inform, educate and entertain'.

10. Scotland: Contract for Britain

In the twentieth-first century, divisions of power and responsibility between the nation state and international institutions are becoming ever more blurred. Indeed, before examining our relationships with countries outside the United Kingdom, it is worth first examining the relationships of the countries inside it.

In May 2011, the Scottish National Party (SNP) won a majority in elections to the Scottish Parliament. First Minister, Alex Salmond, swiftly pledged a referendum on independence, which is likely to be held between 2014 and 2016. The development forces the hand of the UK government in Westminster. While polling suggests inadequate Scottish support for independence during a period of financial hardship, as recently as 2006 an ICM poll found a majority of Scots in favour of independence. Alex Salmond's calculation is that by 2014, with economic recovery in full swing and extended devolution in place, the SNP will be able to convince a majority to support independence from – but close association with – the rest of Britain. How should rest of the United Kingdom respond?

Prime Minister, David Cameron, has made his position clear: 'I will campaign to keep our United Kingdom together with every fibre of my being'. Equally, the coalition agreement pledges to review the West Lothian question (the anomaly that allows Scottish MPs to vote on English matters but not vice-versa), and implement the Calman proposals (on greater fiscal autonomy for Scotland).

Meanwhile, there is rising support for reduction of the level of the Scottish subsidy handed over by taxpayers south of the border to pay for services that are unavailable to the rest of the country. Government spending per capita in Scotland is substantially higher than the rest of Britain. For the financial year 2009/10, the Scots received 67 per cent more taxpayer's money for roads, 65 per cent more on local authority housing, 59 per cent more on social services for the elderly, 44 per cent more on fire services, 9 per cent more on health, 8 per cent more on schools and 5 per cent more on policing. The disparity becomes particularly acute, if you compare funding for services in Scotland with poorer parts of the rest of the UK. In 2009/10, for example, £800 less was spent per person in the North West of England, and around £500 per person less in Wales and the North East. The Scottish subsidy is not based on relative need.

Scottish nationalists point to the revenue derived from North Sea oil – predictably making no discount for the initial UK investment made to get the oil out of the ground. Even then, the net annual subsidy to Scotland has risen from £4 billion to over £10 billion since devolution.

As Britain undergoes a period of austerity, tensions are likely to increase. Attention is now being drawn to the greater services available north of the border – from university tuition (with no fees) to social care. In addition, Scotland relies much more on the public sector for employment.

After his 2011 election victory, Alex Salmond has used more emollient language, stressing the ties that would remain even after independence – from the monarchy to defence. However, having talked up secession, he may find it difficult to reverse his position. A TNS-BMRB Scotland poll for *The Herald*, in June 2011, found a significant swing in favour of independence. Scottish support for the union led by only 45 per cent to 37, with a majority of 18–34 year olds supporting negotiations towards independence.

Just as telling, south of the border, the rising subsidy has fuelled growing disenchantment with the present state of the union. In 2006, a You Gov poll found that 68 per cent of English voters want an English Parliament, and 60 per cent resent the subsidy for Scotland.

Since the referendum will happen in the foreseeable future, Britain needs a positive plan – not just a critique of SNP secessionism. The government should make a bold, honest and comprehensive offer of fiscal autonomy to Scotland as part of a wider 'Contract for Britain', taking into account wider developments in Northern Ireland and Wales.

The enactment of the Scotland Bill in 2011 will take an important step in the right direction, devolving financial powers worth £12 billion per year to the Scottish administration. The 'Contract for Britain' should build on that progress in four important ways. First, it should offer the Scottish executive and Parliament comprehensive tax-raising powers – from income to corporation tax – with an annual payment made by Scotland to Westminster on a per capita basis, to reflect the cost of national expenses, from diplomacy to defence.

Second, in return, Scottish MPs at Westminster would be barred from voting on issues that only affect

England, Wales or Northern Ireland at the committee and report stages of legislation.

The third element of the package would include an end to the UK subsidy to Scotland, with grants and funding to Scotland replaced by local funding, in line with the new fiscal powers.

Finally, the future allocation of revenue from North Sea oil should be referred to a three person arbitral panel, which could in turn make recommendations to Parliament and the Scottish executive. Its terms of reference could be drafted to include due account of relevant geographical considerations and the historic investment made by the British taxpayer.

This deal should be offered to the British people by referendum, in advance of any vote on independence. It should require a double majority of support, in Scotland and Britain as a whole, to succeed. It would force an honest debate about the state of the union. It would offer the Scottish people greater democratic rights – coupled with the financial responsibility that naturally flows from them – while addressing English concerns about the size of the subsidy for Scotland. Above all, it would put the union on a sustainable basis for the future.

SUMMARY AGENDA
- Britain should offer the Scottish executive and Parliament comprehensive tax-raising powers – from income to corporation tax – with an annual payment made by Scotland to Westminster on a per capita basis, to reflect the cost of funding reserved United Kingdom matters.
- Scottish MPs at Westminster would be barred from voting on issues that only affect England, Wales

and/or Northern Ireland at the committee and report stages of legislation.

- There should be an end to the UK subsidy to Scotland – with grants and funding to Scotland replaced by local funding, in line with the new fiscal powers.

11. Defence and Foreign Policy: Delusions of Britannia

Writing in 1997, the former British Foreign Secretary, Lord Hurd, cautioned that in navigating the 'tension between realism and idealism' in our international relations, the policy-maker must 'know the limits of idealism'. The sobering counsel of the realist, which tempered the British perspective in the days after the fall of the Berlin Wall, led from scepticism to despair as genocide ravaged the Balkans and Rwanda, and as newly democratised Russia slipped into cronyism.

In the ten years that followed, Britain's new Prime Minister, Tony Blair, abandoned a realist stance and launched Britain into a period of international hyper-activity. Blair committed Britain to major military interventions in Sierra Leone, Kosovo, Afghanistan and Iraq. He made unprecedented pledges of international aid, produced ambitious environmental targets, joined the International Criminal Court, and sought to forge closer ties with America as well as deeper European integration.

In 2007, the new Prime Minister, Gordon Brown, inherited this long catalogue of overseas ambitions, with Britain poised on the cusp of economic crisis fuelled by government debt. Shorn of the financial means and political will, Britain has fallen short of many of the international goals set during this period of irrational exuberance. With her military exhausted and over-stretched, diplomatic good will impoverished and a currency recoiling from the brink of default, the chasm between Britain's international ends and the means necessary to achieve them has never been wider.

We need a break from the missionary zeal of the Blairite era. Britain in 2011 must reconcile ambition with power. Despite the impact of the most damaging recession since the Second World War, Britain remains uniquely well placed to navigate the peculiar opportunities and risks of an international system that has both globalised and fragmented since the end of the Cold War, producing what US commentator Robert Kagan calls an 'age of divergence'. Britain has deftly adjusted herself to a post-imperial status. She has emerged with a unique combination of strengths – a relatively open free-market economy, a historic commitment to free trade, the capacity to project military force at distance coupled with a nuclear deterrent, the special defence and intelligence relationship with America, an agile diplomatic service, the global dominance of the English language, a network of Commonwealth ties and membership of the European Union. But the lofty Blairite aspiration can only lead to failure – followed by lingering decline – unless Britain either focuses her international goals more sharply, or makes the commitments required to realise them. A policy of 'hit and hope' can no longer be sustained. Britain must choose. It is time for Britain to revive and re-design a conception of the 'national interest' for a twenty-first century foreign policy, around two central tenets.

First, Britain must shed her utopian internationalism, in favour of an international agenda that develops its ends from an assessment of means, rather than vice-versa.

Second, Britain must reprise the habit of viewing foreign policy goals through the prism of a national cost-benefit analysis. International decision-making in the twenty-first century is often indistinguishable from domestic policy, and a determination of the national interest requires government to be able to articulate the tangible gains of the policies it adopts.

Nowhere is the scale of British over-reach more evident than in her military ambitions. None of the stated, or underlying, aims of the invasion of Iraq spoke directly to the British national interest. Saddam was no direct threat to the UK. Wider concerns over his arsenal of weapons of mass destruction proved illusory. Loyalty to the United States failed to secure any real influence on the direction of policy in Iraq, let alone across the wider Middle East. While some dreamed of a new democracy in the Middle East, many British diplomats and soldiers on the ground in Iraq were less convinced.

If the ends were unclear, the means to achieve them were also difficult to discern. The Chilcot Inquiry pointed to a long list of strategic planning failures: the flawed decision to purge the new government of all Baathists, the lack of UK troops in Basra to stop the looting and the reliance on soft-skinned Snatch Land Rovers which became easy targets for insurgents.

The discrepancy between the strategic ends and military means also occurred in Afghanistan. Britain's original aim – along with the US and coalition allies – was a surgical operation to remove al-Qaida fighters from Afghanistan after the 9/11 terrorist attacks. As home-grown Taliban displaced foreign jihadis, those objectives became more opaque. By August 2009, Britain's Foreign Secretary was explaining the NATO mission in the nebulous terms of providing 'effective protection and a better life' for the Afghan people, while the head of the British army listed nation-building, reconstruction and stable governance as part of a strategy that might require a UK military presence for up to forty years.

The humanitarian intervention in Libya, following the UN Security Council resolution 1973, presents a familiar dilemma. Regime change – the only sure fire way to prevent reprisals against civilians – is fettered by the terms of the UN mandate. That increases the risk of stalemate or chaos. This, in turn, may attract terrorist groups to fill the void. Meanwhile, the British public grows increasingly wary of Middle Eastern entanglements that lack well-defined aims and any exit strategy.

These wars illustrate a more fundamental problem. Britain's armed forces are stretched to breaking point by the ambitious objective of bringing Western democracy to inhospitable environments. To have any chance of success the ends must be scaled down, or the resources, the means of achieving our ambitions, should be scaled up.

As the country faces a period of austerity following the recession, Britain faces stark choices. Extensive savings in domestic expenditure must be made both to reduce the tax burden on British business to stimulate economic growth, and to free up resources to sustain current levels of defence investment. Public opinion will not allow any larger scale investment in defence. Nor does history suggest this is necessary – in the first half of the nineteenth century, at the height of Empire, Britain spent between 2–3 per cent of GNP on her armed forces.

A sound economy is the foundation of national security. Cuts in military investment would make the UK much more vulnerable to external threats. Downsizing the Trident nuclear deterrent makes little sense at a time when the number of nuclear rogue states is increasing. Cancelling plans for new aircraft carriers, or the F-35 Joint Strike Fighter designed to fly off them, would substantially weaken Britain's ability to project military force. These considerations argue for retaining an independent nuclear deterrent, a strong infantry and the ability to act in military engagements abroad.

The principal problem remains the UK's over-stretched commitments. Military capacity must be balanced with a much sharper definition of British ambitions abroad. Last year, Britain's military presence in Afghanistan cost £11 million per day in financial terms alone. Given the opaque war aims that the current government inherited, and lack of economic and political progress compounded by a flawed Afghan President, Britain needs the realism to withdraw without further human and financial costs. The major inhibition is the fear of damage to UK-US relations. Yet Britain will be of little long-term value to the US as an ally unless it can sustain its current operational capability, which now necessitates withdrawal – within months not years. Likewise, Britain should resist any further commitment in Libya, and scale back her military involvement in the shortest timeframe practicable.

Britain must adopt a much more critical approach to military intervention, avoiding wholesale nation-building or regime change, without a clear exit-strategy. We should also be very clear about the nature of our national interest in these campaigns. This does not mean the introduction of a more isolationist policy. Rather, by cutting back on open-ended and ill-defined missions, Britain can be more focused and successful in overseas intervention.

There are four discrete areas where Britain should focus her commitment to internationalism.

First, given her global interests and the diverse international threats, Britain must re-affirm the right under international law to self-defence to protect herself from attacks on her territory, allies, citizens and shipping whether by rogue states, terrorist groups, pirates or other non-state actors. Britain and her allies must re-affirm this right of self-defence against possible interference from the International Court of Justice and the International Criminal Court.

Second, there is a case for Britain offering greater support to selected UN peacekeeping operations, as a substitute for the less sharply focussed commitments of the last decade. UN peacekeeping can support the national interest. Paul Collier estimates the cost-benefit of deploying peacekeepers is around £1 for every £4 saved by averting the costs of civil war. Equally, Britain should be able to support limited, surgical military operations, in exceptional circumstances, to prevent a humanitarian catastrophe (as in Rwanda). But, clear and objective criteria would need to be established. The UK should limit itself to well-defined interventions and intervene either decisively or not at all.

Third, Britain should seek to maximise the exercise of its soft power, particularly its diplomatic skills, to wield greater international influence. The pursuit of a more independent-minded foreign policy would strengthen the UK's credibility to resolve international conflicts, from the Caucusus to Kashmir. Nations exercising more independent-minded foreign policies exert disproportionate influence over international affairs, whether it is Norwegian mediators paving the way for the Oslo Accords, or a Swiss Prosecutor putting Slobodan

Milosevic in the dock of an international war crimes tribunal. As Lord Ancram, a former member of the Intelligence and Security Committee, has observed, 'we could do worse than establish ourselves as a major player in this increasingly important field of conflict resolution'. London is already a hub for Alternative Dispute Resolution in financial and commercial disputes. It would be a natural extension for Britain to establish itself as a pre-eminent centre for resolution of international diplomatic disputes. Britain combines diplomatic expertise, excellent universities and the global reach of the Commonwealth. London can be for mediation what The Hague is for adjudication. This would strengthen British influence across a range of international affairs.

Fourth, Britain should be more, not less, assertive in helping nations on the continent of Africa. Africa's exposure to environmental catastrophe, a source of large scale refugee movements, and her fertility as a breeding ground for terrorism and weapons proliferation provide a direct national interest in helping some of the poorest countries. Paul Collier proposes that the West should sign contracts with recipients of aid, to guarantee democracy, good governance, the rule of law and basic standards of human rights. The international community, Collier argues, should ignore coups against corrupt and venal leaders, but intervene to protect those discharging their obligations under internationally recognised 'development and democracy' deals. This proposal merits serious consideration. Britain should work with its partners – including the US, Canada, Australia, France and the Netherlands – to promote such a 'new deal' for Africa. Such a deal would be supported by independent scrutiny of the contractual benchmarks for performance and would include African involvement in any military operations. The objective is not to replace nation building with region building, but to provide surgical external support that can allow the emergence of African success stories, which could, in turn, serve as models of development in the continent.

Overall, Britain's advantage is best served through a flexible strategy, with more peace-making and peace-keeping, and less wholesale nation-building. Such a role would combine Britain's instinctive internationalism with realism, enabling her to act with other powers such as the US and the EU, according to her national interest. It would support Britain's aspiration to promote stability and democracy throughout the Commonwealth and beyond. It is also far more likely to sustain domestic support. In 2009, 65 per cent of adults in the UK believed that Britain's moral authority had been weakened on the international stage in the previous ten years. Yet, 57 per cent of the British public still support the principle of humanitarian intervention.

British efforts to tackle other international problems suffer from a familiar utopian delusion. As if weighed down by post-imperial guilt, Britain has sought atonement in the missionary zeal with which she has embraced international challenges like global warming and aid for developing countries. In both cases, messianic rhetoric has been punctured by a more complex reality.

The UK government has legally pledged to cut CO_2 emissions by 22 per cent (by 2012), 34 per cent (by 2020) and 80 per cent (by 2050). Britain has unblinkingly accepted hugely ambitious targets to cut CO_2 emissions without clear and credible means to deliver them, ostensibly on the twin basis that Britain bears greater moral responsibility for climate change through CO_2

emissions, and that poorer countries are unable to afford to cut their own emissions.

The assumption that 'the rich must pay for climate change' is underpinned by a toxic mix of Marxism and outdated anti-colonial sentiment. Even if British industrialisation were to be viewed something to be paid for, we should also take into account how many other countries benefited enormously from Britain's early industrialisation. Applying international environmental rules retrospectively may be arbitrary – under any principles of natural justice – but it is also misguided.

The more honest reason for richer countries bearing a greater share of the environmental burden is simple – they can. But this makes climate change negotiations a question of charity, in which case – like aid – it depends on the compassion of richer countries. Environmental negotiations perhaps should be a consideration of international development policy.

Tony Blair's strategic mistake was the crude assertion that 'the national interest is to a significant extent governed by international collaboration'. In a democracy, enlightened national interest should drive a country's commitment to global rules, not the other way round. That is not a recipe for inertia. Britain has selfish reasons for cutting CO_2 emissions and contributing to a global effort to mitigate the impact of climate change. Britain needs to wean itself from a reliance on energy from unstable parts of the world, whether from Russia or the Middle East. British firms also have an advantage in developing cutting edge technology that reduces heat from buildings, or pioneering hydrogen fuel cells. Britain should follow the recommendations of its leading engineers like James Dyson, whose March 2010 report set out a range of proposals for financing high-tech companies.

Dyson also proposed investment in the Research and Development that will drive innovation in the growing market for clean energy. For Britain, it makes both environmental and commercial sense.

Perhaps the single most neglected area of policy is 'resilience'. Policy-makers need to recognise that Blair's pledge to 'stop global warming' was delusional nonsense and focus harder on adapting domestic infrastructure to mitigate the impact of climate change, protecting domestic energy supplies, road and rail and strengthening coastal and river flood defences.

While UK environmental policy needs to be focussed on what it can deliver at home, that does not mean that we should ignore international efforts to reach an agreement. The case for helping poorer countries tackle climate change remains compelling, based on humanitarian instinct and a collective sense of responsibility for the planet, rather than some vague theory of natural justice. The developing world contains some of the countries most vulnerable to the natural disasters and extreme weather events that climate change risks inflicting on the planet. So, Britain should continue to participate actively in climate change negotiations. But when Chinese negotiators deny the phenomenon of global warming to resist limits on domestic CO_2 emissions and Indian ones demand £120 billion per year to cooperate in a multilateral deal, it suggests important parts of the developing world take global warming far less seriously than more developed countries such as Britain.

The 1997 Kyoto agreement failed to deliver its goals, the 2009 Copenhagen summit ended in deadlock and the 2010 Cancun conference did little better. It is time to recognise that an international deal without substantial commitment from all major countries to cut CO_2

emissions would be neither internationally fair, nor deliverable at home. Britain should not allow itself to be held hostage to onerous limitations on its economy without an equal commitment from those countries that are set to outpace Western nations in their energy consumption in the near future.

A better approach would be to have international negotiations between the twenty countries responsible for 80 per cent of CO_2 emissions, instead of the 190 governments haggling by committee in Cancun. The G20 would be a far more effective forum to build a consensus on climate change. In the meantime, Britain should increase its bilateral support to help the poorest countries most at risk to strengthen their resilience to natural disasters and environmental threats. This would form part of the UK's international development goals.

The delusional attitude of 'guilt by industrialisation' is echoed in Britain's approach to overseas aid. When it comes to formulating aid policy to help the poorest countries in Africa, Tony Blair famously declared in 2001 that 'the state of Africa is a scar on the conscience of the world. But, if the world as a community focused on it, we could heal it.' Blair backed up his emotive language by raising Britain's spending on international aid and, in 2004, setting up an international commission to propose solutions to Africa's problems such as poverty, a falling share of world trade and a high death toll from conflict, famine and disease. Yet, despite good intentions, these pledges are unlikely to make a real difference.

The most damning indictment recently came from Zambian economist, Dambisa Moyo, who laments the $1 trillion given to Africa from rich countries since the Second World War. Moyo does not just think aid is ineffective. She says it is debilitating. Despairing of current aid policies as a cause of corruption and a driver of a dependency culture, Moyo makes the case for free-trade, micro-finance and the promotion of Foreign Direct Investment as the solid foundations for helping Africans to help themselves. In contrast, Paul Collier criticises – but does not altogether dispense with – aid as a means of policy. He wants it to be focused more sharply, including on technical assistance to support new reforming governments get off their knees, and to help landlocked countries access a coastline.

UK international development policy under the Blair and Brown premierships was largely ineffectual. The establishment of an independent Department for International Development (DfID) dislocated aid from its proper role in support of wider foreign policy goals set by the Foreign Office and often delivered with the military. In Iraq and Afghanistan, this lack of co-ordination led to missed opportunities to fill the vacuum left by fleeing local militias and terrorists. In other contexts, DfID has actively worked against stated British foreign policy objectives. DfID undermined efforts to bring to justice senior members of the Lords Resistance Army in Uganda, for example, who had been indicted by the International Criminal Court for atrocious crimes against children and other civilians.

A lack of strategic discipline has been compounded by DfID's unfocussed approach. By 2010, DfID was spending its budget on 108 different countries, including millions spent on China, just as the Chinese were lavishing £20 billion on the 2008 Olympic Games. DfID did not properly assess the effectiveness of its programs. All the while, Britain is locked into a European network of agricultural subsidies and trading barriers that actually prevent African development.

When it comes to both Britain's international aid and environmental policies, the focus, co-ordination and delivery required bear little relation to the putative ends. Or, as Dominic Lawson wrote in *The Independent*, UK policy 'is a tremendously ineffective exercise in guilt avoidance'.

Britain should overhaul its aid policy around helping the poorest countries build the infrastructure necessary to drive economic growth, good governance and respect for basic human rights. That means a greater focus on technical assistance. It means promoting home-grown solutions and it means doing no harm. Too much aid 'leaks' into military spending – Collier estimates that 40 per cent of military spending by governments in the 'bottom billion' is funded by aid. Bilateral aid should be calibrated – or taxed – so that more goes to governments who spend less on arms.

The range of countries assisted should also be significantly narrowed. In 2009/10 India was the largest recipient of UK aid. Other middle-ranking countries also receive a disproportionate share. Britain needs to review the criteria for aid, and place much greater emphasis on focused help for the poorest.

If the ends need to be more tightly focused, the means to deliver these ends must fit Britain's wider foreign policy strategy. In recent years, DfID has effectively tried to run a shadow foreign policy, driven as much by post-imperial guilt as the national interest. It should be abolished as a separate and autonomous department, with its functions and resources moved to, and reconciled with, the wider foreign policy agenda led by the FCO.

When it comes to fostering Britain's bilateral relations, a changing world should also determine the nature of Britain's relationships.

While the special relationship remains important, it should not trump all other considerations. After all, it doesn't for the US. The US supported a unanimous resolution by the Organisation of American States calling for Britain to negotiate sovereignty of the Falkland Islands, against the democratic wishes of the Islanders.

It is a sign of dwindling UK relevance in Washington that her interests can be dismissed so lightly. Yet, the US is simply adjusting to the global political realities. It is time Britain did the same. Britain must start to see her relationship with the US as reciprocal and flexible, not exclusive and unconditional. In the words of the Prime Minister, David Cameron, the UK-US alliance should be 'solid, not slavish'.

International relations have fragmented since the end of the Cold War, diffusing power among a much wider range of mid-ranking nations particularly across Asia and Latin America. Britain's near-obsessive fixation on the US and EU has distracted relations with the rest of the world. Japanese and Australian diplomats are constantly bemused by the insular focus of European diplomacy, and particularly Britain's neglect of Asia.

In the twenty-first century, British diplomacy needs a much wider network of international partners, to expand its horizons and increase its scope to act independently. Britain should be supplementing her bilateral relations beyond the US and EU across Asia and Latin America. Britain should re-energise its relations with the Commonwealth, harnessing the breadth and diversity of a global organisation bound by the English language and which costs the UK taxpayer just twenty pence per person, per year (compared to EU membership at £52 per person, per year). It offers the opportunity to work more closely with a range of strategically important countries – including India, Canada, New Zealand, Australia, South Africa, Malaysia and Singapore – without any sacrifice of sovereignty. Lord Ancram argues that Britain should formally propose relocating the Commonwealth's headquarters to India, recognising the dynamic potential of the largest democracy in the world, while lessening its London-centred imperial heritage. The proposal should be taken seriously.

Beyond the Commonwealth, other bilateral relations matter enormously. Britain must reinvigorate and reinvest in her bilateral relations around the UK national interest in promoting free trade, expanding democracy and strengthening respect for human rights. It does not mean a dogmatic insistence on Western-style liberal democracy. It does mean 'gearing' her relations according to a set of common values. Britain's overarching strategy should be to seek closer trading, diplomatic and cultural ties with every country that is not engaged in serious human rights abuses. Britain should engage the emerging nations of Asia and Latin America. We should support economic growth and democracy in poorer parts of the world including Africa. We should continue to favour those countries that favour free trade, demonstrate good governance and respect basic standards of democracy and human rights.

This approach sits more comfortably both with British domestic values, and the national interest. At an economic level, it allows Britain to pursue her natural instinct towards global trade liberalisation, while securing market access for British exporters and attracting foreign direct investment. At a political level, it avoids the UK becoming too close to tyrants and despots. This policy supports the broader international stability and good governance and avoids the charges of hypocrisy that have been made in recent years.

If Britain must remain true to her domestic values abroad, she must also replace hubris with humility. Change in foreign regimes will more likely be the result of gradual and consistent pressure, not sudden coercive force. Britain's moral responsibility is to encourage reform and avoid making foreign governments more corrupt or oppressive. We should not hope for instant regime change. Britain needs to adhere to a foreign policy equivalent to Thaler and Sunstein's 'nudge' theory, to reconcile its idealism and realism, developing a strategy that nudges foreign governments to behave more constructively over the long term.

That means learning the lessons of history. Appeasing dangerous despots is both immoral and risky. We need a wholesale repudiation of the maxim that originated with Harry Truman's Secretary of State, Dean Acheson's description of Yugoslavia's Tito: 'He's a son of a bitch, but he's our son-of-a bitch.' Whether it was support for jihad in Afghanistan against the Soviets, Saddam Hussein as a bulwark against Iran, or the premature rehabilitation of Colonel Gaddafi, this morally hollow approach has ended in humiliating failures.

Britain stands at the crossroads. She faces opportunities and challenges in a global climate that is more fluid and unpredictable than at any other time in the last sixty years. Yet Britain has all the capacity to thrive, both contributing to the alleviation of some of the world's most intractable problems, while pursuing its own national interests. Neither old alliances, hyperactive interventionism nor an unthinking supranationalism will provide the foreign policy Britain needs.

Clumsy and naïve internationalism must give way to a more rugged internationalism, one that combines the values of a good global citizen with the realism to assess the credibility of British aspirations and commitments abroad. Above all, Britain requires a more independent-minded foreign policy, measured against both her values and her resources, her ends and her means. Britain needs a fresh policy that is prepared to act when the means to deliver are present, and to desist from action when the national interest or will is not.

SUMMARY AGENDA

- Britain must develop a more independent-minded foreign policy, working with the US and our European partners, but with a broader global outlook that takes due account of other rising nations, particularly in Asia and Latin America.
- Britain should adopt a more rugged internationalism, balancing its responsibilities as a good citizen in the world with the national interests of its taxpaying citizens.
- The UK's foreign policy goals must be more consistently reconciled with the financial, military and political means to achieve them.

12. Europe: Making a
Two Speed Union Work

The European Union and the Conservatives

If there is one thing we have learned from the 2011 debt crisis in the eurozone it is that the fears of the eurosceptics about the euro currency were largely right. Monetary union is impossible without eventual fiscal union. Fiscal union in turn is impossible without democratic assent.

The current shape of the union looks fundamentally unstable: either it becomes much more fiscally united, or it breaks apart.

These are momentous decisions. If we are to influence the future life of the union, we need to have our own agenda. Unfortunately, like their European counterparts, UK politicians are all too aware that their own Europhile views are not shared by their constituents. The easiest way to deal with the problem is to ignore the issue entirely, thus making sure, almost by definition, that anyone who tries to bring the issue of Europe into the national debate is caricatured as an 'obsessive'.

But this conspiracy of silence is increasingly unsustainable as well. As the new coalition government is rapidly discovering, the EU simply has too much influence on our domestic politics to be eternally ignored. Extensive regulation from the EU creates new red tape slowing down UK business, while its laws and courts constrain the ability of our politicians to follow their own judgments.

These problems look set to get worse in coming years. Already, elites in the EU are seriously talking about the possibility of tax harmonisation and extending new regulation to curb the supposed excesses of the financial sector. A Britain with more of its laws sets by the EU will almost certainly be a more statist Britain.

The legacy of the Lisbon Treaty was to convert the European Union from an institution based on common agreements and opt outs, to one based on central control and Qualified Majority Voting. The inconsistencies in the current structures are clear. The EU now has three presidents: the President of the European Council, the President of the European Commission and a Presidency of the Council of the European Union.[146] Between these presidents, the division of power and responsibility remains obscure. The nature of any institution tends to cause it seek to gain more power. There is little barrier now to the EU's continual quest for more control.

In purely financial terms, our net contribution to the EU takes up an increasing amount of our budget. While domestic government across the continent imposes difficult cuts everywhere, there seems to be little effective pressure across the EU to restrain its growing size. Under the current budget proposals, funding will increase by at least 7 per cent from €1013.8 billion to €1083.3 billion between 2014 and 2020. Between 2000 and 2020 that represents a 23 per cent increase in real terms payments

---

146 Technically this is a country, and rotates on a six monthly basis.

from €112.2 billion to €138 billion (in today's prices). Around 42 per cent of that budget is dedicated to the Common Agricultural Policy, the Common Fisheries Policy, and rural development.[147] The UK will contribute €12.9 billion to the 2011 budget.[148] In the last two years, our annual contributions have already gone up by more than 60 per cent. It is notable that while the expenses crisis brought British politics to a halt, few have noticed that each MEP currently cost the taxpayer five times as much as any MP.[149]

But this is just one aspect of the problems the EU has always faced, the lack of democratic accountability. The fundamental ideological objection to the EU has always been that while Europe may be a geographical entity, it lacks a 'demos'. Its people do not feel part of the same nation. They are not ready to debate and compromise together over common problems and solutions.

The result is that the day to day decision making in the EU gets ignored – at least until a nation is asked to make a sacrifice for its neighbour. The end result is a chronic lack of connection between the elites at the apex of the EU project and those electorates they are supposed to be serving. This fissure continues to grow. The democratic relationship between politicians and voters now seems terminally dysfunctional.

It is a cliché to remark that few people could tell you who their MEP was. But, perhaps fewer than we might like could tell you who their MP was either. On

---

147   Commission proposal for the EU budget post-2013: the good, the bad and the ugly, Open Europe, 2011

148   http://www.civitas.org.uk/eufacts/OS/SF1.htm

149   http://www.openeurope.org.uk/media-centre/pressrelease. aspx?pressreleaseid=111

the other hand, most would have some idea of who the Prime Minister was, of what party was in power, of what central policy reforms they had attempted, and whether they were considered to be a success. None of these same conditions can be said of the EU itself.

The supporters of the EU are perhaps right that we now live in an increasingly globalised world. Britain is no longer, if it ever was, an island alone. We must pursue our interests and values through the flawed international institutions and relationships that do exist. Cooperation is becoming essential.

But that doesn't mean we necessarily always have to pool power solely on a geographical basis. There is minimal domestic debate – parliamentary or public – on the tangible pros and cons of the increasing number of European measures in social, justice and home affairs policy. European integration has become an end in itself, rather than the means to achieve a particular aim.

EU integration has increasingly stretched its democratic mandate to breaking point. The Lisbon Treaty was forced through, despite the rejection of the original EU Constitution by referenda in two of the most traditionally Europhile countries, the Netherlands and France. Meanwhile, the Eurozone has proved unable to withstand debt crises. There exist underlying structural imbalances between richer and poorer European nations, which pose serious doubts over its continuing viability – and the willingness of German taxpayers to bail out its more profligate members.

Similar attempts have been made to elide the differing foreign policy priorities of the EU's twenty-seven members. Bureaucrats at the European Commission have long yearned to answer Henry Kissinger's quip: 'If I want to call Europe, who do I call?' However, the formation of a European External Action Service, building a European diplomatic corps and forging a single foreign policy, cannot mask profound differences in approach to international affairs. Meanwhile, the creation of four posts vying for power and influence over the direction of EU external relations only exacerbates the fractious nature of Europe's foreign policy decision-making.

The crisis in the eurozone and the forthcoming deadline for Britain to opt out of the ECJ jurisdiction over the EU Justice and Home Affairs agenda by 2014 offer Britain an opportunity to seize the initiative. Britain's history, values and outlook are distinct. Britain's commercial instincts sway heavily towards membership of the union, but its distinct liberal – as opposed to social democratic tradition of individual liberty, and its unique justice system and long history of independent engagement in world affairs put Britain on a slightly different path.

The best relationship for Britain, other member states and the EU as a whole, would allow for 'variable geometry', or a 'multi-speed' Europe. This would be based on membership of the common market, but would allow the freedom to opt out of social, justice and foreign policy.

In contrast, Gordon Brown's Foreign Secretary, David Miliband, articulated the case for a single European foreign policy – and closer EU integration – in terms of preventing international relations being dominated by a 'G2' of China and the US. This approach neatly exposes a delusion of British foreign policy. On the one hand, Britain's influence in world affairs is reduced to its ability to influence the direction of an enlarged EU of twenty-seven member states. On the other, it arrogantly reduces international relations to three 'powers that count', shrouded under the misguided impression that the EU can – collectively or as a single power – steer the course of world events. The Miliband doctrine is telling in another respect. Miliband openly advocates a balance-of-power approach. He just calculates that Britain will better maximise her interests via the EU – a calculation not supported, unfortunately, by any experience.

As a nation, Britain has always been suspicious of the EU project. The vision of a United States of Europe does not appeal. We did well to stay out of the euro, and to secure a rebate. Nevertheless, as a country we are not yet ready for complete withdrawal. The British people still want to see if we can make the project work. We want to enjoy the benefits that exist of working together, to secure a friendly alliance of countries together in a free trade area.

No club appreciates members who never make a positive contribution and only whine in the background. If we are to stay part of the European Union, we should have our positive vision for its future. Simply trying to slow down integration isn't enough.

In which case, what should our agenda be?

It has long been evident that in practice a two speed European Union already exists. Rather than slide into it reluctantly, Britain should seek to lead the debate on how best to make it work.

This looser arrangement would encourage Britain to cooperate with her European partners on a range of common challenges – from counter-terrorism to climate change. If the sovereign debt contagion precipitates more EU treaty negotiations, it will present the ideal opportunity to shape such a two speed Europe originally conceived at Maastricht in 1992. This Europe would be based on different groups, cooperating on diverse issues, at differing levels of intensity.

Take the example of trade. Whereas Britain was once a driving force in support of free trade, there is now virtual silence as Britain is tied by the negotiating prerogatives of the EU Commission at the World Trade Organization (WTO). Britain and other EU member states have given up the right to negotiate in favour of striking a common position that the European Commission can adopt in any world trade talks.

Yet the expansion of free trade internationally – led in no small part by President Clinton during the 1990s – has stalled. In practice, the EU remains one of the most strident of protectionist voices at trade talks. The EU is impeded by its internal policy, the sclerotic Common Agricultural Policy (CAP) of subsidies and support that consume almost half of the EU budget, protecting inefficient European farmers from outside competition and tying British farmers up in bureaucracy and red tape. Food and farming is Britain's largest manufacturing industry and should be seen as an area for export growth. The current policy hurts British (and European) consumers, who suffer from artificially high food prices. It leads to retaliation from other countries, notably the US, leading to a downward spiral of beggar-thy-neighbour protectionism.

President George W. Bush barely nudged the US towards a new WTO free trade deal. President Obama has struck an even more protectionist note. In a marked shift in US consensus, all of the last US Presidential nominees (except John McCain) campaigned on more or less protectionist platforms. On the European side, hopes for a new deal were vested in an unlikely advocate for free trade, Peter Mandelson – a former Young Communist– who, despite his best efforts, found himself hemmed in by Europe's agricultural lobby.

On either side of the Atlantic, who today is prepared to champion free trade? Britain should campaign energetically for reductions in trading barriers – on principle, as well as national interest – but has lost her independent voice. In an increasingly multipolar as well as multilateral world, British interests would be better served by treading a more independent path, divergent from both the US and the EU.

The reason behind the EU Commission negotiating trade deals is the link between external trade negotiations and the EU's internal commercial policy. But why should Europe's internal rules fix international policy, rather than vice-versa? It should be perfectly possible for EU member states to take independent positions at the WTO and agree that any final deal reached would bind them domestically and within the EU. No other region of the world adheres so rigidly to a single negotiating position. Members of other free trade areas, such as the North American Free Trade Agreement (NAFTA), have not sacrificed their individual voice at the negotiating table. In contrast, they negotiate autonomously at the global level. They simply stick to other regionally-agreed rules.

Trade policy is a good example of a case where pooling national sovereignty, has failed to deliver a better overall outcome for Britain. The UK has tied her hands, giving up the means to pursue one of her most important foreign policy ends – one that serves UK interests, the global interest and some of the poorest countries in the world. Never has such an important common international goal been so readily sacrificed for the narrowest of special interests unrelated to the British national interest.

In the aftermath of the failure at Doha, national governments are furtively exploring the scope for bilateral trade and investment deals. Such avenues remain closed to Britain – merely for the sake of the illusory benefits derived from a common EU external trade policy.

Britain must wrest back control over her foreign policy decision-making. That would allow her to develop an international trade policy that advances British interests, from broader trading access for its financial services, manufacturing and IT industries to the consumer's interest in cheaper food and other commodities. At the same time, British championing of trade liberalisation would help the poorest nations in the world.

Beyond external trade, Britain has given up control of many of the rules that govern her own internal markets. As part of the Lisbon Treaty, the Charter of Fundamental Rights, was incorporated into EU law. This text, in effect a miniature constitution, sets out fundamental political, social and economic rights for citizens. The worry is that such an ambiguous law can be used by activist judges to create costly new regulations. During the Lisbon negotiations, Britain tried to secure a separate protocol that the Charter would not create any new justiciable rights in the UK. It remains to be seen whether this will be legally sufficient.

Already the new law from EU regulation has created significant costs for UK businesses and consumers. Between 1998 and 2010, regulation cost the UK economy £176 billion. £124 billion of this came from EU legislation, and £38.9 billion alone from employment legislation.[150] There is no reason to assume that these costs will go down. By far the most expensive piece of regulation

---

150   Gaskell, Sarah and Persson, Mats, 'Still Out of Control? Measuring eleven years of EU regulation', Open Europe, 2010

is the Working Time Directive, and this has already been extended eight times by the European Court of Justice.[151]

There is no real reason for pooling sovereignty on such employment law. The appropriate regulation for any country largely depends on its political and industrial culture. The same regulation is highly unlikely to suit such diverse systems as the Scandinavian nations, Germany and Britain. Britain should seek to restore its own control on this issue, strengthening its current, somewhat tenuous, opt out.

Besides this, Britain will soon be forced to make a definite decision on two other crucial areas.

In 2014, Britain will have to decide once and for all whether it wishes to opt out of the jurisdiction of the European Court of Justice over the EU Justice and Home Affairs agenda. Coordination among international police forces is certainly desirable, but giving away sovereignty over criminal investigation altogether is a step too far.

Britain will also likely have to make a stand on is financial regulation. In the wake of the financial crisis, the EU looks set to attempt to arrogate as much power as possible over financial regulation. While Britain is dominant in the EU in terms of financial services, we will struggle to defend the City of London given our limited voting rights.

Again and again in different policy areas we see a similar pattern. The EU is trying to create a common culture in our employment law, in our justice system, our foreign policy, our trade negotiations and our financial regulation. Yet this common culture does not really exist. It is as artificial as the common currency proved to be.

---

151 Repatriation of EU Social Policy: The right focus for a Conservative government, Open Europe, 2009

Britain should be unafraid to stress the areas where cooperation benefits everyone, and the areas where decisions are better made on a national level. This need not be a negative agenda. Such a loose union would be easier to expand. Expansion has always been one of the key historic successes of the European Union, encouraging human rights and development. As a leader in the new 'Europe lite', Britain could press harder for the entrance of new member states such as Turkey.

The future of the European Union is in flux. While the pieces are still in play, Britain should take the chance to decide what it is exactly that she wants.

SUMMARY AGENDA

- Rather than simply complain about the European Union, Britain should seek to put forward a positive contribution on how best to make a two speed Union work.
- Britain should seek to regain control over its criminal and social law, its financial regulation, farming and fishing policy.
- Britain should not let its membership of the European Union stop it from campaigning more vigorously internationally for freer trade and forming its own trade deals.

Conclusion

This book is not a manifesto; it does not purport to be a comprehensive programme of policy for the next Conservative government. On the other hand, it aims to accomplish more than a mere political pamphlet, which might simply give a broad direction without prescribing any policies. *After the Coalition* is consequently something of a hybrid. It does offer some policies in key areas, as well as offering a broad path along which future policies may be developed.

We are conscious of the many omissions and policy areas we have not tackled in the course of the book. We are aware that issues concerning local government and the development of technology could have been treated by the book. We are conscious that some would want to have read more about climate change. Fashions in policy debates change, and what may seem insignificant to one commentator may be another's life mission. Rather than offering a comprehensive plan for government, the book aspires to stimulate further debate on a range of important questions, while giving some policy ideas rooted in the Conservative tradition. As authors, we are all Conservative Members of Parliament who have sought to further the interests of the party we represent after those of our constituents. There is no shame in this. As modern Conservatives, we do not feel that the Conservative Party needs to offer any apology for its beliefs or for its record in government.

A modern Conservative Party should consequently be at ease with itself, confident that it can lead policy debate in Britain without having to be overly-reliant on focus groups. The authors of this book have a traditional view of politics, in which politicians campaign on clear platforms and attempt to persuade the electorate to adopt their policies. Different parties have different policies which they attempt to sell to the electorate, rather like competition in the retail sector. Over the past twenty years, however, this model of politics has replaced by a scheme in which politicians compete to find out what the voters want, and then tailor their message to what they believe the voters' preferences are. This approach has been typified by the focus group, in which a group of key voters is asked their opinion on various subjects. This approach has the benefit of actually involving voters, ordinary members of the public in decision making. It suffers, however, from the drawback that the electorate is increasingly volatile and prone to changing its mind.

It also takes away much of the responsibility from the politician. A truly focus-group driven politician, if such a creature existed, would simply echo what the people wanted. There would be no place for political leadership or vision, as these have been understood in the western democratic tradition. It would result in politicians being utterly irresponsible, in the strictest sense of the world.

Responsibility has been an underlying theme of this book. At the beginning of the book, we looked at fiscal responsibility and the possibility of imposing unambiguous rules by which public spending could be regulated in the future. Such discipline is highly responsible and contrasts vividly with the profligate spending and borrowing of some Western governments in the first decade of the century. The book then moved on to growth strategies which affirmed the principal role the private sector plays in growth, in contrast to the more profligate State. Responsibility once again underlay our commitment to public services, where we argued that an ageing population and a poor fiscal position would lead to individuals taking a greater role in social provision. Next, we looked at how responsibility for learning could be returned to our schools, their teachers and their pupils.

This new emphasis on responsibility on the part of governments and citizens is only one indication of the shifting circumstances in which modern countries find themselves. The twentieth century saw an enormous accretion to the power of governments, as two World Wars of unprecedented scale, bloodshed and expense were fought. To prevail in both the First and Second World Wars, the Allied powers borrowed and spent on a gargantuan scale. With the increased size of government during the twentieth century came a belief in 'cradle to grave' provision of services, that governments were all-powerful and that individuals could do nothing to better their own circumstances. The state was all-providing and all-powerful.

The ongoing problems with sovereign debt have discredited the high spending, high debt cultures which led, in many cases, to a fiscal mess which may yet overshadow the strictly financial sector difficulties of 2008. The State, we argue, simply got too big to pay for itself. This was masked in times of prosperity, but when the good times stopped, the enormous spending commitments in terms of welfare pushed many developed countries to the point of bankruptcy.

The current troubles have also served to reveal what had been long cloaked by the economic good times: in many areas, Britain is currently heading in the wrong direction. While we are all proud of our country, we should not be afraid to point out areas where we believe other nations are doing better. We can learn from the work ethic and educational performance of the Asian tigers, the business ethos and free spirit of the US or the economic reforms in South America. Britain's relative decline in the face of new economic and political powers is not inevitable. For too long we have not have not held our governments, our institutions and the individuals in our society properly accountable for their own actions.

It is in this context that the notion of responsibility – a greater sense of discipline and judgement on the part of governments and individuals – becomes so important. The fiscal distress of the last few years was caused by a lack of responsibility – an indulgent spree of expenditure without care for the consequences. Greater responsibility shown by governments and individuals will lead to a more prosperous future. It this wider hope which has animated our efforts in writing *After the Coalition*.

After the Coalition – Book in Brief

1. Values and Priorities

- Individuals, organisations and governments need to take more responsibility for the success and failure of their own actions.
- We need to challenge today's cultural consensus that free markets, profit and competition are inherently bad. These virtues lifted Britain and much of the rest of the world out of poverty, and into the modern era.

2. Economy

- Over the course of an economic cycle, Britain should run a balanced budget. We should never be running persistent deficits when the economy is growing faster than 2 per cent a year, its long run trend.
- The Office for Budgetary Responsibility should be the final arbitrator for what government spending is counted as investment. It should release an annual report setting out Britain's full debt commitment, including its pension commitments, PFI deals and so on.

3. Business
- Our tax system should be simplified and reformed, taxing consumption and pollution rather than savings and hard work. We should bring forward the coalition's plan to lower the rate of corporation tax to 23 per cent to the 2012 Budget
- We should seek new funding for vital infrastructure, such as new transport, energy and communications networks. At the same time, we should reform planning laws to make it easier for businesses to grow the economy.
- We should reform union laws to require a majority of support from union members before a strike can proceed.

4. Environment
- We should use market mechanisms such as a Carbon Tax to tackle the challenge of climate change, rather than increased government planning and bureaucracy.
- We should have a strong plan to upgrade our roads and airports.

5. Welfare
- We need to end the 'hand out' culture. We should introduce greater conditionality and time limits into the welfare system.
- We should establish a new 'Right to Own' principle within our social housing sector.
- We need to create a welfare system more in accordance with the fluid nature of modern employment. The government should create a new Baby Bonus, instead of maternity pay. We should create

new tax incentives for those who look after the elderly in their own home.

6. Health

- We should continue the current successful reform programme in the NHS, allowing successful hospitals to expand and weaker hospitals to close. We should take advantage of the extra efficiencies private sector companies can provide.

- We should seek to improve the quality of end of life care. In particular, we should make sure all patients are given the chance to discuss their own individual preferences for their quality of death early as possible.

7. Education

- We should expand the current free school programme, allowing such schools to make a profit.

- A core general education including maths, science, English, history and languages should be compulsory to sixteen. An ABacc should be developed to provide a 'college track' for bright students from all backgrounds with a strong technical alternative.

- We should seek to end grade inflation through the creation of a single examination board 'owned' by the top universities.

- Students failing to achieve the required level should be 'held back' a year. Fast progressing students should be accelerated through school courses.

- We should give schools more powers to dismiss failing teachers and reward better their strongest performers.

8. British Justice: Firm but Fair

- We should restore public confidence in the justice system by seeking longer, tougher prison sentences. These would not only better protect the public, but give the offender more of an opportunity for rehabilitation.
- A robust policy of transferring and deporting foreign national prisoners coupled with the transfer of the mentally ill to secure hospitals would ease pressure on the prison estate and free up places for serious and persistent criminal offenders.
- The remainder of England's prisons should be contracted out to the private sector on a payments by results basis, reducing the bills for prisons by at least 15 per cent.
- The prison regime needs to be overhauled so our jails are not simply human warehouses, but constructive regimes that promote work, training and alcohol and drug rehabilitation.
- We should create new 'Enterprise cards', setting strict quota limits on the immigration of both EU and non-EU workers.

9. Civil Liberties

- We should create a Bill of Rights that protects Britain's tradition of liberty, enshrines meritocracy and restores democratic control over the wider human rights agenda.
- We should reform media regulation to preserve freedom of the press and promote media pluralism

in the new digital age. A new 'thin BBC' should return it to its original mission to 'inform, educate and entertain'.

10. Scotland

- Britain should offer the Scottish executive and Parliament comprehensive tax-raising powers – from income to corporation tax – with an annual payment made by Scotland to Westminster on a per capita basis, to reflect the cost of funding reserved United Kingdom matters.
- Scottish MPs at Westminster would be barred from voting on issues that only affect England, Wales and/ or Northern Ireland at the committee and report stages of legislation.
- There should be an end to the UK subsidy to Scotland – with grants and funding to Scotland replaced by local funding, in line with the new fiscal powers.

11. Defence and Foreign Policy

- Britain must develop a more independent-minded foreign policy, working with the US and our European partners, but with a broader global outlook that takes due account of other rising nations, particularly in Asia and Latin America.
- Britain should adopt a more rugged internationalism, balancing its responsibilities as a good citizen in the world with the national interests of its taxpaying citizens.
- The UK's foreign policy goals must be more consistently reconciled with the financial, military and political means to achieve them.

12. Europe

- Rather than simply complain about the European Union, Britain should seek to put forward a positive contribution on how best to make a two speed Union work.
- Britain should seek to regain control over its criminal and social law, its financial regulation, farming and fishing policy.
- Britain should not let its membership of the European Union stop it from campaigning more vigorously internationally for freer trade and forming its own trade deals.

Bibliography

Reports and Articles

Akiba, M., et al., 'Teacher Quality, Opportunity Gap, and National Achievement in 46 Countries', *Educational Researcher*, 36 (7), 2007

Alberta Education, 'Education – Annual Report 2010/11', 2011

Ambler, Tim and Boyfield, Keith, 'Reforming the Regulators', Adam Smith Institute, 2010

Balling, Bruni and Llewellyn, 'The Failure of Northern Rock – A Multidimensional Case Study', 2009

Barlow, James and Burn, Jamie, 'All Change Please', Policy Exchange, 2008

Bogdanor, Adam, 'Not Working: Why Workfare Should Replace the New Deal', Policy Exchange, 2004

Booth, Philip, 'Getting Back Your Health', Adam Smith Institute, 2002

Bosanquet, Nick, 'A Successful National Health Service', Adam Smith Institute, 1999

Bosanquet, Nick, et al., 'A Lost Decade: Counting the Opportunity Cost of Public Spending 1999–2008', Reform, 2008

Bosanquet, Nick, et al., 'Making the NHS the Best Insurance Policy in the World', Reform, 2008

Bosanquet, Nick, 'Fewer Hospitals, More Competition', Reform, 2010

Bosanquet, Nick, 'The NHS in 2010', Reform, 2004

Bosanquet, Nick, de Zoete, Henry and Haldenby, Andrew, 'NHS Reform: The Empire Strikes Back', Reform, 2007

Bosanquet, Nick, Haldenby, Andrew and Rainbow, Helen, 'Fit for Recovery', Reform, 2009

Boys Smith, Nicholas, Martin David and Kay, Lawrence, 'The Cost of Complexity: How Britain's tax system strangles the economy and reduces British competitiveness', Policy Exchange, 2008

Browne, Anthony and Young, Matthew, 'NHS Reform: Towards Consensus?', Adam Smith Institute, 2002

Butler, Dr Eamonn, 'Re-Booting Government: How to deal with the deficit without cutting vital services', Adam Smith Institute

Butler, Dr Eamonn, 'Why Britain Needs an Economic Responsibility Act', Adam Smith Institute

Cawston, Thomas, et al., 'Old and Broke: The Long Term Outlook for the UK's Public Finances', Reform, 2011

Cawston, Thomas, et al., 'Productive Parents', Reform, 2009

Cawston, Thomas, Haldenby, Andrew and Nolan, Dr Patrick, 'The Money-Go-Round: Cutting the Cost of Welfare', Reform, 2010

Cawston, Thomas, Haldenby, Andrew and Nolan, Dr Patrick, 'The End of Entitlement', Reform, 2009

Centre for Social Justice, 'Dynamic Benefits: Towards Welfare that Works', 2009

Charlson, Paul, Lees, Christoph and Sikora, Karol, 'Free at the Point of Delivery – Reality or Political Mirage?', Doctors for Reform, 2007

Clark, Tom and Dilnot, Andrew, 'Long-Term Trends in British Taxation and Spending', IFS, 2002

Clark, Tom and Dilnot, Andrew, 'Measuring the UK Fiscal Stance since the Second World War', IFS, 2002

Corkindale, John, 'The Land Use Planning System: Evaluating Options for Reform', Institute of Economic Affairs, 2004

Crawford, Rowena, Emmerson, Carl and Tetlow, Gemma, 'A Survery of Public Spending in the UK', IFS, 2009

DCSF, 'A Code of Practice on the Provision of Free Nursery Education Places for Three- and Four-Year-Olds', 2006

Department for Work and Pensions, '21st Century Welfare', 2010

DfE, 'The Importance of Teaching: The Schools White Paper', 2010

DfE, 'School Workforce in England, November 2010 (Provisional)', 2011

Diggle, Paul and Ormerod, Paul, 'Be Bold for Growth', Centre for Policy Studies, 2010

Elphicke, Charlie, '10 Points for Growth', Centre for Policy Studies, 2011

Evans, Alan W. and Hartwich, Oliver Marc, 'The Best Laid Plans: How Planning Prevents Economic Growth', Policy Exchange, 2007

Featherstone, Henry and Evans, Natalie, 'Controlling Public Spending: The NHS in a Period Tight Funding', Policy Exchange, 2010

Featherstone, Henry and Storey, Carol, 'Which Doctor? Putting Patients in Control of Primary Care', Policy Exchange, 2009

Featherstone, Henry and Whitham, Lilly, 'The Cost of Cancer', Policy Exchange, 2010

Gaskell, Sarah and Persson, Mats, 'Still Out of Control? Measuring Eleven Years of EU Regulation', Open Europe, 2010

Goldhill, David, 'How American Healthcare Killed My Father', *The Atlantic*, September 2009

Goldsmith, Michael and Gladstone, David, 'Road Map to Reform: Health', Adam Smith Institute, 2005

Green, David G., 'Response to the DWP Consultation Document: 21st Century Welfare', Civitas, 2010

Haldenby, Andrew, et al., 'Off Balance', Reform, 2011

Hawkins, Nigel, 'The Party is Over: A Blueprint for Fiscal Stability', Adam Smith Institute, 2009

Helm, Dieter, 'Utility Regulation, the RAB and the Cost of Capital', University of Oxford, 2009

Helm, Dieter, Wardlaw, James and Caldecott, Ben, 'Delivering a 21st Century Infrastructure for Britain', Policy Exchange, 2009

Hodgen, et al., 'Is the UK an Outlier? An International Comparison of Upper Secondary Mathematics Education', Nuffield Foundation, 2010

House of Commons Education Committee, 'The English Baccalaureate', HC 851, Fifth Report of Session 2010–12, Volume I: Report, Together with Formal Minutes, Oral and Written Evidence, 2011

The Howard League for Penal Reform, 'No Winners: The Reality of Short-Term Prison Sentences', 2011

Hutton, Will, 'Review of Fair Pay', Interim Report, 2010

IMF, 'Macro-Fiscal Implications of Health Care Reform in Advanced and Emerging Economies', 2010

Institute for Fiscal Studies, 'Tax by Design - The Mirrlees Review', 2010

Kerr, Sari Pekkala and Kerr, William R., 'Economic
    Impacts of Immigration: A Survey', Harvard
    Business School, 2011

The King's Fund, 'A High-Performing NHS? A Review
    of Progress 1997–2010', 2010

Knighton, Brochu and Gluszynski, 'Measuring Up:
    Canadian Results of the OECD PISA Study:
    The Performance of Canada's Youth in Reading,
    Mathematics and Science: 2009 First Results for
    Canadians Aged 15', Statistics Canada, 2010

Lamb, Norman, 'The NHS: A Liberal Blueprint',
    CentreForum, 2010

Leunig, Tim, 'In My Back Yard: Unlocking the
    Planning System', CentreForum, 2007

Lilico, Andrew and Sameen, Hiba, 'Taxation, Growth
    and Employment', Policy Exchange, 2010

Lilico, Andrew, Holmes, Ed and Sameen, Hiba,
    'Controlling Spending and Government Deficits',
    Policy Exchange, 2009

Lilico, Andrew, O'Brien, Neil and Atashzai, Adam,
    'Controlling Public Spending: The Scale of the
    Challenge', Policy Exchange, 2009

Llewellyn, John and Dharmasena, Bimal, 'Conditions
    for Growth', Centre for Policy Studies, 2010

Machin, Stephen and Vernoit, James, 'Changing School
    Autonomy: Academy Schools and their Introduction
    to England's Education', 2011

Martin, David, 'Benefit Simplification: How, and why,
    it must be done', Centre for Policy Studies, 2009

McKinsey & Company, 'How the World's Best
    Performing Schools Systems Come Out on Top', 2007

Ministry of Justice, 'Breaking the Cycle: Effective
    Punishment, Rehabilitation and Sentencing of
    Offenders', 2010

Morgan, Patricia, 'The War between the State and the Family: How Government Divides and Impoverishes', Institute of Economic Affairs, 2007

Morgan, Tim, 'Five Fiscal Fallacies', CPS, 2011

Morton, Alex, 'Making Housing Affordable: A New Vision for Housing Policy', Policy Exchange, 2010

Moulton, Jon, 'Pain Aversion', CPS, 2009

Moyes, Bill and Corrigan, Paul, 'Future Foundations: Towards a New Culture in the NHS', Policy Exchange, 2010

Murray, Alasdair and Wilkes, Giles, 'Fiscal Rules OK?', CentreForum, 2009

Newmark, Brooks, 'The Hidden Debt Bombshell', CPS, 2009

Niemietz, Kristian, 'A New Understanding of Poverty: Poverty Measurement and Policy Implications', Institute of Economic Affairs, 2011

Niemietz, Kristian, 'Transforming Welfare – Incentives, Localisation and Non-Discrimination', Institute of Economic Affairs, 2010

Nolan, Dr Patrick, 'The Fairness Test', Reform, 2011

Norridge, Eve, 'Implementing GP Commissioning', Policy Exchange, 2011

Oakley, Matthew and Saunders, Peter, 'No Rights Without Responsibility', Policy Exchange, 2011

Oakley, Matthew and O'Brien, Neil, 'Tackling the Causes of Poverty: Replacing the Child Poverty Target with a Multi-dimensional set of Causal Indicators', Policy Exchange, 2011

O'Brien, Neil, 'Just Deserts? Attitudes to Fairness, Poverty and Welfare Reform', Policy Exchange, 2011

Open Europe, 'Commission Proposal for the EU Budget Post-2013: The Good, the Bad and the Ugly', 2011

Open Europe, 'Repatriation of EU Social Policy: The Right Focus for a Conservative Government', 2009

Protti, D. and Johansen, I., 'Widespread Adoption of Information Technology in Primary Care Physician Offices in Denmark: A Case Study', The Commonwealth Fund, March 2010

Quarmby, Katharine and Fazackerley, Anna, 'Building Blocks? An Investigation Into Building Schools for the Future', Policy Exchange, 2009

Rally Against Debt, Fact Sheet, 2011

Ramsay, Cynthia and Butler, Dr Eamonn, 'Medical Savings Accounts', Adam Smith Institute, 2001

Reform, 'A Better Way', 2003

Reform, 'An NHS for Patients, 2011

Reform, 'It Can Be Done', 2011

Reform, 'Why the NHS Needs Real Reform', 2002

Romer, Christina D., 'Macroeconomic Policy in the 1960s: The Causes and Consequences of a Mistaken Revolution', 2007

Saltiel, Miles, 'No Need to Flinch: The need for NHS Reform', Adam Smith Institute, 2011

Selzer, Dr, 'A Review of Privatisation and Regulation Experience in Britain', Institute of Economic Affairs, 2000

Sinclair, Matthew, 'Wasting Lives, a Statistical Analysis of NHS Performance in a European Context since 1981', Taypayers' Alliance, 2008

Smith, David B., 'Living with Leviathan: Public Spending, Taxes and Economic Performance', IEA, 2006

Smith, Dominic, 'Public Confidence in the Criminal Justice System: Findings from the British Crime Survey 2002/03 to 2007/08', Ministry of Justice Research Series 16/10

Smith, Ian, 'Building a World-Class NHS', Reform, 2006

Sumner, Scott, 'The Case for NGDP Target: Lessons from the Great Recession', Adam Smith Institute, 2011

The King's Fund Briefing, 'Health and Social Care Bill', 2011

Triggs, Matthew and Bowman, Sam, 'Welfare Reform: The Importance of Being Radical', Adam Smith Institute, 2010

Wilkes, Giles, 'A Balancing Act: Fair Solutions to a Modern Debt Crisis', CentreForum, 2009

Willlman, John and Smith, Martin, 'Innovation and Industry: The Role of Government', Policy Exchange, 2009

Wolf, Alison, 'Review of Vocational Education – The Wolf Report', Department for Education, 2011

Young, Peter and Saltiel, Miles, 'The Revenue and Growth Effects of Britain's High Personal Taxes', Adam Smith Institute, 2011

Books

Clark, Gregory, *A Farewell to Alms* (Princeton University Press, 2007)

Cowen, Tyler, *The Great Stagnation* (Dutton Adult, 2011)

Glaesar, Edward, *Triumph of the City* (Penguin, 2011)

Gruber, K. H., 'The Impact of PISA on the German Education System', in Ertl, Hubert (ed.), *Cross-National Attraction in Education: Accounts from England and Germany* (Symposium Books, 2006)

Harford, Tim, *The Undercover Economist* (Hachette, 2006)

Katz, Lawrence F. and Goldin, Claudia, *The Race Between Education and Technology* (Harvard University Press, 2008)

O'Toole, Randal, *Gridlock* (Cato Institute, 2009)

BIBLIOGRAPHY

Rosewell, Bridget, *Planning Curses: How to Deliver Long-Term Investment in Infrastructure* (Policy Exchange, 2010)

Wellings, Richard and Lipson, Briar, *Towards Better Transport* (London: Policy Exchange, 2008)